The Reverend Anthony H. Denney, after twelve years of parish experience, served for eight years (1962-70) as Research Officer of the Church of England Children's Council. He is the author of *Children in Need* (SCM Press 1966)— a subject which has been one of his special concerns—and he contributed an important appendix on "Religious Education in Special Schools" to the recently published *Durham Report** sponsored by the Church of England Board of Education and the National Society. He is now vicar of Lower Shuckburgh, Daventry.

The Library of Pastoral Care

TITLES ALREADY PUBLISHED

Library of Pastoral Care

WORKING WITH CHILDREN

Working with Children

A. H. DENNEY

LONDON

S · P · C · K

1971

First published in 1971
by S.P.C.K.
Holy Trinity Church
Marylebone Road
London N.W.1

Made and printed in Great Britain by
William Clowes and Sons, Limited
London, Beccles and Colchester

SBN 281 02467 7

Contents

Acknowledgements

Thanks are due to the following for permission to quote from Copyright Sources:

The Pergamon Press: *Lord of the Dance*, by V. R. Bruce and J. P. Tooke

1

Pastoral Care

The Church's ministry to children has undergone quite radical change in the last decade. This change has been in part a reflection of changes in both educational and theological understanding, and in part a response to the very different social conditions in which children are growing up today from those to which their parents and grandparents were accustomed.

It is commonplace today to recognize the changes that have taken place in family and community life; father's role in the home has extended and he spends more time in active care of his children than was generally so a quarter of a century ago; mother on the other hand has proportionately decreased her involvement in "home" and extended her outside activities to community and work, particularly after her children have begun school. Grandparents are less involved with the children owing to mobility and housing differences between the generations; the extended family which is still a feature of life in the older areas of large towns is becoming increasingly rare. Higher standards of living make family outings and family holidays a frequent possibility and the car makes families less dependent upon the community in which they live; many housing areas are little more than dormitories. Sunday is a day out for the family and church-going, when it is practised, need have no more local obligations than shopping. All these factors and many more which have been the subject of social studies demand that ministry shall be flexible, ready to depart from conventional patterns, and constantly ready to adapt itself to local conditions and change as they change.

Between 1840 and 1940 the generally accepted pattern of the ministry to children remained unchanged. The Sunday Schools of the nineteenth century had, necessarily, to change from places of general education, as their name implies, to places of exclusively religious education. It was in these establishments that ministry, apart from baptism and burial, found its chief place of expression. The training of children in a Christian way of life and in prayer was the task of the parent or governess; the teaching of catechism and scripture was often carried out in complete isolation from the activities of the adult congregation. It was left to the numerous sects and societies, of which many grew up in the last decades of the nineteenth century, to exercise a care which extended beyond the ministry of teaching. Behind this situation lay a number of assumptions which few church members would have questioned. The family, at least the middle-class family, could be relied upon to fulfil its educational role in the Christian upbringing of children, its values would be transmitted, its habits and obligations inherited; at least until 1914 it was a stable group in a stable society. The content of religious instruction was clear; it was printed in black and white in the Book of Common Prayer where it had remained, almost unchanged, for three and a half centuries. It was, and indeed still is, an admirable summary of necessary doctrine in the traditional pattern of Christian theology. The majority of teachers' handbooks for use with children in Sunday Schools were based upon the Catechism. The influence of progressive educationists was small, though teachers trained in Froebel method did have some impact. Most of the available literature came from theologians rather than from educationists.

The years following the war of 1939–45 revealed many of the defects of this traditional system. Allegiance to the Church declined among young people, parents and children alike. The system was inflexible, Church-centred and backed by very little educational expertise. In spite of the work of St Christopher's College from which most of the diocesan advisers in religious education came, and in spite of the publishing activities of the Church of England Children's Council, the fall-off continued. By the beginning of the sixties it was clear that the traditional pattern of ministry and the traditional content of teaching were both unsuited to changed conditions and new educational insights. A group of research workers,[1] each working independently in his or her chosen field, began to turn attention upon the child, his capacities, his way of developing and learning, his emotional and social needs, his way of life, and the many influences and pressures to which he is subject and how he reacts to them.

With these new insights a fresh conception of ministry is emerging. A clearer understanding has come of how children learn, and consequently material has been offered which is more suitable to them at different developmental stages. The importance of relevance has been recognized and the association of faith with experience has made selections and adaptations within the vast field of Christian theology, both traditional and modern, so as to meet the child's needs in the complex society in which he lives. It has been recognized that the ministry to children is a ministry to the whole child in every facet of his growth and experience; it is a ministry that cannot be exercised unless the whole child is considered and unless the pastor makes every effort to know his sheep.

This is not a "how to do it" book; there are many excellent books of that kind available, of which several are listed in the relevant places here. It is rather a presentation of the child to the pastor so that he may make a beginning in "knowing his sheep". It suggests ways of pastoral care which may be new to some, "old hat" to others, but which will aid the sheep in knowing and trusting their shepherd. If it seems to have too much of the child in it and too little of God, this is simply because experience suggests that those for whom it is written are already "men of God" but are often seeking for ways in which to communicate the love of

[1] See book list for Chapter 1 in "Books for Further Reading", p. 111.

God, which they know, to the children of whom they are
very aware that they know too little.

In so small a volume as this only a tentative beginning
can be made. It is hoped that the books listed will help in
extending the subject matter of each chapter.

2

Child and Home

Every child is the product of his parents and his home. It is only in the context of the family that a child can be properly understood. The child whose parents are unknown and whose home is the streets or the fields, or whose provider is the state or a voluntary society, proclaims these facts as clearly and stridently as the child of devoted parents and a happy and generous home.

This inseparability of the child from the family can be easily forgotten in the anxiety of those who are responsible for seeing that his needs are met. Teacher, minister, doctor, social worker, psychologist, and many others, are at one time or another concerned with the child's needs, yet no one of them can assess the needs that are his special responsibility without considering the family from which the child has come. Yet unfortunately, and sometimes necessarily, there is little opportunity of meeting a child in his family setting. Teachers cannot hope to have more than a sketchy background knowledge of their pupils' home life. Such knowledge as they are able to glean is often second-hand from the child himself, coloured by the child's pride or shame, his reluctance to expose the "nakedness of the land"; or his eagerness to be the same as or even better than his school friends may lead him into fantasy or exaggeration. Visits of parents to school add substantially to the picture, but teachers' visits to homes are few and far between and cannot, in present conditions, be expected to be much else.

A great deal of what we try to do in the schools is wasted because we have too little understanding of our children's environment. Some of us tend to see the school as an island of culture in a sea of barbarism. Our speech, our dress, our values, set us apart from our pupils and their homes. We do not usually live where they live—"All some of us know of the neighbourhood is the quickest way to the nearest bus stop", as one Headmaster said to me. There are few "Miss Reads" and no village shops in Stepney, Salford, or Smethwick.[1]

There is a strong awareness among social workers today that the child in trouble spells the family in trouble. No effective treatment can be given unless the child is seen in the family context and his difficulties interpreted in the light of knowledge of his family situation. Heavy case loads, a shortage of trained workers and financial considerations often make this awareness very difficult to implement in terms of an adequate family service.

> We are now beginning to realise that personal relationships and attitudes are basic to every type of lack, failure, or dissatisfaction with which we try to deal. The recognition of the overriding importance of the family and of the ways in which it can be supported, modified and strengthened by caseworkers and residential staff is now pointing the way towards the establishment of a Family Caring Service.[2]

The pastor, no less than other professional persons concerned with the needs of children, will want to know as closely as he can the family circumstances of the children to whom he ministers. It is in the family that the ministry to the child begins. Frequently children will become known in ways that are not immediately associated with the family, as, for example, the open club, the church services, cadet groups, uniformed organizations, and so on. Children in need of special attention will be known through social agencies, children's homes, training centres, special schools in the parish. In all these instances children may be known, indeed very well known, without any specific reference being necessarily made to their homes and families. Though much important and effective pastoral care can be exercised

[1] *Parents and Teachers, Partners or Rivals?* Lawrence Green. Allen & Unwin

[2] *The Community's Children*, ed. Jessie Parfit. Longman

in these situations, full understanding will only be possible if opportunity can be made for home visiting. The magnitude of this task in a large and active parish is fully appreciated. It raises large issues of staffing and the most effective use that can be made of lay members of the church. This will be touched on in later chapters; at present it must be emphasized that the size of the task does not lessen the need to appreciate its importance and to search for the means of putting it into practice.

MOTHER AND CHILD: THE FIRST TWO YEARS

Before looking at a few of the reasons which make the family such an important factor in understanding children one thing must be said which will bear upon all study of children's varying needs as they grow up. While we rightly stress the importance of the family as the place of security, nurture, education, and love, it must always be seen also as the point of departure. The child is nurtured in order to become independent and mature. This process begins when the infant is weaned and continues throughout the whole span of his growing life. Watch a child newly introduced to a playgroup. John, aged three, is the second child of the family, his sister has now started school, and mother is looking forward to an hour or two of morning freedom and so has hopes of John's acceptance of a local play group. Mother is advised to stay in the hall for the first few sessions while John gets used to his new surroundings. At first John remains close to mother, absorbed in the activities around him but a non-participant, a fringe observer. The sand table, the water trough, the large bricks fascinate, but not enough to overcome the fear of separation from the security of mother. Twenty minutes pass in this state of tension, then John makes a sally to the sand trough and digs his fingers in. A well-meaning adult helper proffers moulds and a shovel; immediately John is back with mother. But not for long; a further and longer sally is made with backward glances to ensure the continuing presence of his mother.

An attack from another child, a shower of sand, sends him scuttling back. On the next venture out John is enjoying a new found experience; attack results in his replying in kind. By the end of the third session mother's presence is unnecessary and by the middle of the second week he cannot get his outdoor clothes off fast enough to begin play.

Writing about "Affectional Bonds" John Bowlby, who has done so much work on the mother-child relationship, writes:

> In humans attachment behaviour is probably at its most striking during the second and third year of life. At that age young children most of the time prefer to be within sight or sound of a familiar adult whom I shall call the child's mother-figure, or mother for short. Though a young child often makes excursions further afield, he will tend also to return. Moreover, if mother moves a short distance away he will usually try to follow her and, if she goes too fast, will protest by crying. When mother returns after a short absence he is likely to greet her with a smile, to approach her, and as likely as not to indicate, by the well-known gesture of raising his arms, that he wishes to be picked up. The ordinary devoted mother is more than familiar with all these sequences, and plays her complementary role. As a result mother and child are usually not far from one another.[1]

Not all children will react with this sort of adaptation; some take longer, some a shorter time. Some never quite make the real break for freedom that is hoped for, but more about these later. Some lessons can be learned from this example of mother-child attachment. First, mother is a point of departure as much as a place of security. The security she offers is vital to the growing child, but he is always moving from it. What the mother represents is protection against the unknown world outside. This unknown world, however, is as essential to growth as the known world of home. To provide the facilities for exploration of the unknown world in an atmosphere of security is therefore a joint function of both home and community. Furthermore the example showed that John was seeking protection

---

[1] *Affectional Bonds: their nature and origin.* John Bowlby. Paper read at the 7th International Congress on Mental Health. August 1968

from the well-known adult—his mother. John will need similar well-known adults in the community if he is to find the sort of protection which is at present represented by mother.

In his mother the growing child finds a protector who is also someone who loves him, whose protection includes many extras which are reflected in attitude, voice, and treatment as well as other roles not necessarily protective. Yet it is significant that children who receive treatment which is actually hostile and far removed from loving will cling tenaciously to "home" against the fearful threat of removal to an unknown, however physically pleasant, environment. Nurture and familiarity produce a sense of safety of a sort, even if it is little more than a bolt-hole, a port in a storm; and to the growing child life is a veritable storm.

Attachment to "home" is not, however, just a matter of familiarity. As we shall see later, when looking at the child's early development, the mother-child relationship is so close in the early months of life that for a time she, who is his entire world, is indistinguishable from himself. Indeed for the first two years or so of his life the child finds it difficult to identify himself or to acquire any consciousness of self. The word "I" does not appear in his vocabulary until about this time. He will often talk about himself by name rather than by a personal pronoun. This growth in self realization is accompanied of course by the realization of other "selfs" around him, of which the mother is the most prominent. These "selfs" will be endowed with the same qualities as himself. This is the beginning of a recognizable love relationship. Before this stage is reached, though mother will treat her baby as a person, he will not be able to respond to her as a person, his responses being almost exclusively ego-centric. But now his dawning recognition of other "persons" will enable such reciprocation to take place.

The many different ways in which a mother expresses her attitude to her child are admirably set out by John and

Elizabeth Newson in their studies of infants and four-year-olds in an urban community.

NEWSAGENT'S WIFE:

"Oh yes—when he comes to me for love he gets it. I don't ever push him away or say he is a big boy or that sort of nonsense, because he *wants* loving, and I love him because I do love him."

And the four-year-old reciprocates.

ACTOR'S WIFE:

"Yesterday, for instance, I was in a state. They were all yelling and screaming and everything, and I hadn't washed, and she suddenly looked round and said "Oh mummy, you *do* look lovely!" And I said, "Oh Juliet, I wish I did!" and she said "You look lovely to me"—and this was very thrilling that she said this.[1]

FATHERS AND OTHERS

This same pattern will be followed in the child's adventure beyond the mother, but there will be significant differences. While the recognition of mother as a person has been a long steady process of separating her first from himself and then from the rest of the world around him, the discovery of other persons in the family will not have this long pre-history. Father, brothers, and sisters have never, in his mind, been identified with himself; they are and have always been other than himself. This otherness may be a strong factor in the child's early religious development. In writing of the relationship of father and child Roy Lee has this to say:

Because the father is separated out from the objective mother and not from himself, he is always *other* to the child, always something of a stranger and an alien to him. This sense of "otherness" is reinforced in the child by his relations with the father in the next few years ... at this point we can anticipate the conclusion and say that our conception of the person of God is a development of the young child's conception of his father. One of the popular descriptions of God is that he is

[1] *Four years old in an urban community*, John and Elizabeth Newson. Allen and Unwin 1968

wholly "other". We can see the reason for this in the way the child first realises his father as a separate person.[2]

Although father is usually the closest person to the child after his mother, other members of the household, child or adult, receive due recognition and have to be "discovered" and explored. Just as the relationship with father is a vital part of the child's growing consciousness, so also are the other members of the family. While they do not affect his emotional development quite so radically, yet the response they offer to his explorations will be a strong determinant in his ability to continue them beyond the family circle.

This brings us back to John in his play group. Here he will meet most probably the first adults beyond the family, with whom he may establish an intimate relationship. Within the family, first with his mother, then with father and other members of the family, he will have felt outwards for a loving response. Love will at first be patterned upon what he has expected to receive and has received from his mother. As he grows in awareness of other people he will learn what particular contribution they are able to make to his needs. Frequently they will be temporary substitutes for mother's care, at other times they will have their special role. But at all times the infant's expectations are ego-centric. Though to a diminishing extent, this egocentrism will continue until he is past his seventh birthday. This will be discussed in later chapters, but for the family he is likely to be throughout this period a demanding person whose greatest need is constant affection and patience. He is a very dependent creature, though from three onwards he can be weaned from his dependence by such means as play-group, nursery school, and, from five, the infant class of his primary school. The success of the weaning process will depend to a great extent upon the steady and consistent development of the growing child's experience of adult response.

His mother will have provided the first understanding of

[2] *Your Growing Child and Religion*, Penguin Books 1965

love that he has. The demands that he makes upon her are of course total. To him in his first two years of life she is, as we have seen, almost his whole world. His complete dependence means that only from her can he expect relief of his discomforts and fulfilment of his needs. His awareness of his father introduces a third element into his consciousness, moreover an element that is competitive as well as loving. His first experience of self-discipline is the hard lesson of sharing his mother, a lesson that may be reinforced by other members of the family. He will learn that he is not in full and absolute command of every adult in his environment, but as he tries to sort out the position of each he will do so with expectation of response which is based upon past experience. If his outreach is rejected or aggressively repulsed he will tend to rush back to the known sources of care. Fear and frustration will be proportionate to degrees of rejection experienced and the possibility of alternative sources of satisfaction. If there are no avenues of escape and no secure place of retreat, the damage to the personality can be very considerable. The young child who is sent away to school before he has gained an adequate degree of self-reliance or is asked to submit to a discipline beyond his experience can suffer more agony than those responsible for his well-being would care to imagine. To be left alone, even for a brief time, in a strange environment from which there is no escape can have an effect which will result sometimes in months of disturbed behaviour. We shall see something of this when we discuss the child in hospital.

WHAT IS A "FAMILY"?

It might be well to conclude this section with some attempt at a definition of what we mean by "family". Any definition we find is bound to be open to objections of one sort or another. If we limit it to the immediate or nuclear family of mother, father, and siblings, the objection is immediately made that this excludes such intimate persons as grandparents or uncles and aunts. If this extended family is received as part of the definition there is the objection that these persons may live so far away as to be almost total strangers to the child, playing less part in his life than the local shopkeeper or the postman.

We have seen above that for the infant the significant persons in his world of experience are those upon whom he can and does call for the satisfaction of his needs, physical or emotional. These people who are so related to him that they fill this role are for all our purposes his family. Whether or not they are, as is usually the case, his blood relations is really beside the point. They may include close family friends, foster parents, child minders—whoever they are, if for the infant they fill the role we have outlined, they are his family. A similar definition has been suggested for social workers concerned with the family and who need to see it whole as the unit in which each member grows and lives:

> The various configurations of possible family meaning for patient and social worker suggest the need for a more functional—and at the same time more adaptable—definition of the family than we encounter in the literature. The writer would like to suggest that a family exists when people related to one another by blood or the sharing of a home consider themselves resources for one another on a more comprehensive basis and at higher degree of intensity than they consider other people.[1]

It is easy to object to this definition as to any other definition, and the first to object may be the parents of the child themselves, who are naturally jealous of their parental role. But for the pastor it may be the sort of definition which will be a good beginning for thought about Christian pastorate as it is concerned with children and as it stems from Gospel precept.

THE PASTOR AND THE FAMILY

The pastoral implications of what has so far been said are fairly evident and there is little need to spell them out in

[1] *Social Work with Families*, ed. Eileen Younghusband. Allen and Unwin 1967

any great detail. It has been the tradition, whether by accident or design it is difficult to say, for the ministry to the family to centre upon the mother. We have seen that there is plentiful justification for this. Unfortunately such centering has tended to go on when the mother is no longer filling a maternal role and it has consequently lost proportion. However it is clear that the early ministry to the child must consist of support for his mother. Such support begins in marriage preparation, but this volume is not concerned with this particular ministry. But support must begin during pregnancy. This is not to say that the emotional condition of the mother at this time affects the child. This is something about which very little is known. But it is the period when the mother together with other members of the family can be helped to a realization of the new set of relationships and responsibilities in which they will shortly be involved. Unless a child is assured of acceptance, his infant life may be less than it should be in the terms we have discussed above. Adaptation to a changed pattern of life does not always come easily to both parents, and there are tensions which will need to be resolved as well as many perfectly sensible questions that will need to be answered.

Some of the best ways of relief and of answer will be found in the uninhibited discussion of the young wives' group with the sympathetic attendance of the physician or midwife. Fathers should not be forgotten in this preparatory stage. The emotional tensions and breakthroughs that occur during pregnancy are normally carried within the relationship of husband and wife, but to be ready for them is to be doubly armed, and the help of a wise gynaecologist to discuss them from time to time can be a great help. Within a very short time the father's role in relation to the growing child will be of tremendous importance and this is only too frequently a point of failure. As often as not the failure is due more to ignorance than to neglect. In later chapters we shall have cause to refer to the father's role and the child's identification with him and the sometimes disastrous effects of failure in this respect. In our society there are still

areas of strong matriarchal authority, but even here there
is growing awareness of the place of father in child rearing
and a growing desire on the father's part to have his share
in the children's care. Any pastoral concern for the child
should include discussion of the part that fathers are playing in modern family life. The growing custom of family
outings at the week-end, whatever it may mean in terms of
Sunday observance, far outweighs in its positive advantages
any disruption it may cause to churchgoing traditions.

THE NEED FOR ACCEPTANCE

It is axiomatic that acceptance of the child from birth, indeed before birth, is essential to his physical, emotional, and
spiritual growth. Luckily there are few mothers who do not
love their child, and few fathers who, even with some initial
tremors, are not delighted and proud with each new arrival.
Where this is not so the pastor has a task before him.
Rejection may be so determined that he will need to bring
in expert help, but often its causes do not go too deep for
normal care to bring them to the surface and so help to
dispel them. Causes of rejection may be post-natal depres-
sion, which brings with it a feeling of incapacity to cope,
unwanted pregnancy, the feeling that the child is a threat
to the career ambitions of the mother, economic stress.
Each of these has its solution which the family as a whole
must be helped to discover. Parental rejection of the infant
whether by father or mother may be the result of more
deeply rooted troubles than these. There may be difficulties
in personality development which stem from the parents'
own rejection in childhood or fears and anxieties which
have quite unconscious origins. Pastoral care and counselling may uncover some of these, but according to the depth
and intensity of the rejection expressed the pastor will decide
how far his own ministry can meet the needs of the family and
at what point the help of the professional skill of the psycho-
therapist should be asked for. Rejection may be the result
of the interruption that the infant causes in the normal sex

life of the parents. Wakeful nights, the strain that breast-
feeding can produce, may make the mother tired and un-
responsive. As a result she may feel inadequate and unfairly
torn between the demands of her husband and her baby.
An experienced pastor may sense this, but it may well be
with her doctor or a therapist that she would prefer to discuss it, and who will best help her to work it out. The
pastor's care will always be in the context of his parochial
ministry; he is not a clinician or a therapist; his insights
are those of a man of God who cares for his people as their
father in God and he will not attempt the methods of
diagnosis that require the training of the specialist in other
fields than his own.

Acceptance of a child depends to a great extent upon a
married couple's ability to accept one another. This in turn
depends both upon past experience of acceptance and
present experience within the immediate community of
living. Supporting and strengthening the family will be
part of the total parochial programme of making some
reality out of the concept of the body of Christ. This raises
the whole complex problem of the ministry in the amor-
phous urban parish of today and takes us far beyond the
limits of this book. Pastoral care however must always be
based upon the recognition of God's acceptance of people
as people, an acceptance which it is the purpose of all
Christian ministry to reflect. The certainty of personal
worth, of personal capacity to contribute, and the recognition of the unique value of each contribution, are criteria
for assuring that the acceptance these standards imply will
be felt throughout the community in which they are
evidenced.

The following brief case history illustrates the way in
which a sensitive parish priest recognized the needs of a
family and through the sacrament of Baptism was able to
offer the pastoral care that was needed:

Angela's baptism: A family was called upon during house to
house visiting. The husband explained that his wife was out
pushing their daughter Angela in a chair. She was almost four

years of age and evidently subnormal. Both parents had been very upset at her condition but, although the father thought that they should have more children, his wife refused. Angela had not been baptized. The father thought that she should be baptized, like everyone else, but they had moved following a change of work and, in any case, he regarded this as more his wife's concern and she had done nothing. The parents did not normally go to church at all.

When the wife was seen on a subsequent visit, it became apparent that this was no simple matter of delayed baptism. It was in fact almost six weeks before the wife could bring herself to discuss the situation with a real openness. She had been unfaithful to her husband and was not wholly certain that the child was his. She felt that Angela's condition was a punishment and cared for her with a painful mixture of affection and atonement. When at last she had told her story she was afraid of being rejected. Indeed she had taken the risk of revealing everything because she had felt that she must confess that it was not Angela's condition as much as her own that prevented her from doing anything about baptism. It was some time before she really believed that both Angela and herself were loved by God and the Church. Her realization of what was involved in baptism helped her not only to see her daughter afresh, but also to see herself anew and trust herself to a loving God.

At this stage the husband came round to say that his wife had told him everything, that they were standing together and wished to have their daughter baptized. They were seen on three evenings one week and the baptism duly took place. Just before the ceremony the wife asked for and received sacramental absolution and set free a right relationship between herself and the other members of the family and God. It was as a result of this that the parents were able to make a proper use of expert help in their care of Angela.[1]

[1] *Number Unknown*, ed. A. H. Denney. C.I.O. 1965

3

The Pre-school Years

In the previous chapter we have discussed some of the factors that need to be thought about in planning the ministry to the very young child in his home. One point that was stressed was that home and parents are a point of departure as well as an environment of love and security.

Readiness to depart will show itself when the young child begins to take an interest in other children of his own age. This interest is at first rather an objective curiosity not unlike that expressed in a new and interesting toy. It is only after some preliminary play in which each child remains separate or in occasional conflict with others that playing together really begins. Piaget[1] describes well the chatter of kindergarten children in a classroom. Each is engaged on a separate task in which he is passionately interested. He will talk to himself, to the thing he is making or doing, to the world in general, but very seldom to any other single child. There is very little talk that is really conversation. Such social contact as arises is usually over the acquisition of some material or tool which is wanted and someone else is using—hence conflict. This stage of self-interest and isolation precedes the further stage at which children become playmates. As play develops and becomes increasingly complex and imaginative the advantage is discovered of involving others in the play situation —at first selfishly and later with a growing awareness of the pleasure to be found in companionship and shared activity.

So we can see four stages in the growing child's recogni-

[1] *The Language and thought of the Child*, J. Piaget, R.K.P. 1965

tion of those who are outside the closed world of the home. First we see mother and child as we have outlined in the previous chapter—a unit consolidated by the needs of the dependent infant; next the interest expressed in other children without any real recognition of them as persons; then play which is physically together but only shared through the common objects of play, as colouring materials, toys, sand tray, and so on; finally the discovery of shared play and companionship.

This development is anxiously watched by parents as it marks the beginning of independence and the opportunity for a little parental relaxation. At last for a little time each day as opportunity offers, through nursery school, play group, a visit from a friend, or a visit to a local playground, it is possible to relax the vigilance and attention which the wholly dependent infant has so far demanded. This development also marks, for all others concerned with children, the time for planning the reception of children into the community away from their parents. It is therefore the point at which pastoral care for children in groups must begin.

WHAT THE PASTOR CAN EXPECT
FROM THE YOUNG CHILD

More will be said later (chapter 4) about learning development and its implications. For the present something must be said about what the pastor can expect from this age group and so what opportunities there are for a ministry to the child apart from his parents.

Whatever is attempted for these very young children will be absolutely crucial for their future development. This is the one intimidating fact that the pastor and his co-workers must recognize. That many clergy attempt very little apart from the kindergarten department of the Sunday school may be some indication that they do in fact recognize this and avoid it because of inadequate resources. The child is testing out a new found world beyond the garden gate—a world of adults and other children who are mostly unfamiliar. He is at a stage of development in which emotions govern him with an intensity which precludes any real control over his behaviour. He needs space and freedom as well as a sense of security—commodities often in short supply in many modern living conditions. He needs good solid safe play materials—expensive items for the average family budget. He also needs the skilled supervision of an adult who understands his needs. It is for all these reasons that the pastoral care of the pre-school child is likely to be more demanding than that exercised for any other age group. At this period particularly, as indeed throughout the whole age range preceding adolescence, the pastor should consider carefully the possibilities offered by other agencies concerned with the child's welfare.

Parish groups responsible for children often express—in different ways—an anxiety about the content of what the Church offers the child. There is felt to be some necessity to offer something which can be seen to be "religious". Thus, if children are to be read to, it is desirable that suitable biblical story matter shall be found for them; if they are to sing it should be hymns or choruses; if they mime or act it should be a biblical theme or tale; finally it is essential that they shall worship God and this should be done in formal and—according to adult standards—reverent manner. Now if this, or some modification of it, is part of the pastor's expectation of the possibilities of care for pre-school children, he is liable to be disappointed. Indeed this sort of expectation of any child is likely to bring disappointment and difficulty. There are two main reasons for this. First there is a failure to distinguish between verbal articulation and emotional experience; secondly there is the imposition upon the young child of adult patterns of behaviour, thought, and expression which are totally irrelevant, indeed very largely impossible, for the young child.

Our expectations of a child at any age, must measure up to the stage of development which the child has reached. This stage, though open to certain reasonably reliable generalizations, is variable for each child. In some children, for example the children of middle-class professional people, verbal development will seem advanced, social development apparently retarded. Quite the opposite may be true of the child of a working class family; his vocabulary will be more restricted, his ability to sit and listen to a story rather more limited, but his social awareness and independence considerably advanced. Each child is therefore to be known, discovered, and understood as an individual. Only so can any effective care be offered to him. This is axiomatic for any skilled teacher and must be equally so for the pastor. However, both pastor and teacher have to deal with numbers of children, often far too many. One of the major problems of caring effectively for the very young is the breaking of the large number of children into manageable small groups.

But to return to the two points raised above. Some decision must be taken about a critical question of the interpretation of experience. For the articulate adult who has a substantial vocabulary, a knowledge of the language of theology, however elementary, and, above all, ready ability to think in and handle abstractions, it seems the most natural thing in the world to put religion into words, to express in verbal terms the content of personal faith and sentiment. The happy adult may "look" happy, smile, laugh, chatter, or even sing. He is unlikely to clap, run madly around the garden, swing on a swing or rope, or throw a ball and chase wildly after it. The young child is very likely to do one or all of these things because it is a great deal easier for him to express his feelings through his body than by words of which he has only a limited supply. Not being able or wishing to understand his emotions in any intellectual fashion he has no wish to put them into words. He acts what he feels in a free and spontaneous way. He also plays and fantasizes his emotions as a means not only of expressing them but of working through them and gaining control over them. It is therefore principally in terms of emotion and physical expression, play and fantasy, that we must expect the young child to express and develop his religious consciousness. Once we have come to an acceptance of the inappropriateness of verbal response we are in a position to explore the possibilities of a right pastoral care for the pre-school child.

DEVELOPING RELATIONSHIPS: THE PLAY GROUP

First, a distinction must be made between the care that is proper to the home situation and that which is needed outside the home. Presuming that the home background is known, care can be assessed in terms of those needs which the home cannot meet. If the home is one in which the ordinary degree of physical and emotional care is being adequately given then the child's needs outside the home will be mainly social. If normal needs are not being adequately met then special attention must clearly be given to them. This is the subject of later chapters, and much may be comprised under the heading of marital guidance or care for an overworked and tired mother. This is beyond our scope at present so we must assume a normal situation. The child's need for extended social contact will be at two levels—peer group (children of his own age) and adult. We have already seen that social contact with his peers is gradual, moving from isolated play in a group context towards companionship as an enjoyable experience in itself. It is this gradual process that makes the play group the ideal situation for meeting this particular need. If properly managed and adequately provided no pressure need be placed upon the newcomer to join in immediately, nor is he so placed that other children will be affronted or other parents put out if there is no response from him. He can play selfishly without being reprimanded, but with just enough conflict from time to time to lead him towards shared play and then to definite relationships with other children of his own choice. These are the sort of advantages which the play group offers over the friendly visit to another child's home.

Adult relationships can also be satisfied through the group. Staffing is a constant problem but with care and co-operation from parents, leader and helpers can establish a one to four ratio with the children, which not only provides adequate supervision but also the sort of close attention to the needs of individual children which are so important a part of care at this age.

This all brings us back again to the question of content. Is our play group, if it fulfils all the ideals suggested above, a means of communicating the faith to the young child? Since we have the children in a supervised situation is not this the opportunity to begin to feed in religious concepts and vocabulary? Some groups indeed attempt this along the lines referred to—chorus songs, stories, pictures, and so on. This may have some successes, but often it represents rather the satisfaction of adult conscience than anything particularly significant for the child. Distinction must be drawn between the experience in which the child is involved and the adult rationalization of this experience in verbal terms of one thought pattern or another, one set of technical terms or another. Such rationalization which associates experiences and forms them into systems with names and relationships, that incorporates concepts of time, quality, comparative values, and persons past and present, will all come at the right stage of the child's development. At the pre-school stage this is fruitless. The important fact is the experience itself and its incorporation into the child's growing awareness of the world around him. His experiences at this age are both foundations for the future and reference points for his growing intellect. The pastor must be satisfied for some time to come to leave them as they are and not try to do the child's learning for him.

This, of course, is not to say that the experiences which the child undergoes in the play group should be left to chance. It is possible, not only by the recognition of staffing qualities but also by careful attention to programme and to equipment, to ensure that the children have the opportunity of learning through their play and slowly gathering the vocabulary which relates to their experiences. The association of words and phrases with immediate experience is the best way in which children can acquire the concepts which will be necessary for later learning stages. This association comes through the adults seizing every opportunity to interpret feelings and relationships with appropriate words. When a child can say "Jane has taken my trowel" he will be better able to cope with his feeling of anger and frustration than if his only means of recovering the trowel is to grab or fight for it. Equipped with "I have banged my leg on the climbing frame" a child can get attention for his hurt more efficiently than standing still and crying. The gradual accumulation of the language which enables urgent matters to be communicated relieves tension and frustration so giving time for more creative experiences to take place. It also provides the groundwork for the later handling of concepts which is important in religious and moral development.

Apart from attention to language the pre-school group can enjoy many experiences at second hand through well-told stories. Here again participation by mime, speech, song, and action can associate verbal expression with activity and "happenings" in a way which prepares for later, more complex concepts. Understanding of "I am sorry", "I forgive", "I make up", "my fault", "I share", "I give", "I receive", "I thank", can be effected by identification with story material. The most important part of the story time is the preparation that the play leader has put into it in choosing material in which identification is possible, in working out the physical accompaniments to the story and the words associated with it. The story also facilitates imagination which is the vehicle of a young child's fantasies. The ability to fantasize is an essential element in therapeutic play. Imagination depends—as the word itself indicates—on the possession of a range of assimilated images which, taken from reality as the child has perceived or experienced it, can be manipulated to fit the patterns which delight, fascinate, or terrify the child; and can also enable him to change reality in such a way that he masters it and works through it instead of being its helpless victim.

The right choice of apparatus and play material on or around which the child's fantasies can be moulded is part of the careful planning which the play group demands.

TAKING STEPS TO FORM A PLAY GROUP

The initial work involved in setting up a play group is not as simple as it might seem. There are legal formalities which must be dealt with and there may even be substantial research among the local possibilities for accommodation before the legal requirements can be met. Play groups come under the provisions of the Day Nurseries and Child Minders Registration Act of 1948 with the addition of the requirements of section 60 of the Health Services and Public Health Act 1968. So it is essential, right from the start, to recognize that play groups are not part of the responsibility of the Education Authority.[1] It is therefore necessary to contact, personally if possible, the Local Health authorities. Generally speaking the authorities are sympathetic towards the establishment of play groups, but must fulfil the requirements of the acts under which they work.

When the premises have been decided they must be inspected by the health authorities and the permission for so using them granted by the Town Planning Committee. For this latter purpose quite detailed plans of the position of the premises may be required. The ideal requirements within the premises will include such things as one w.c. to every ten children, one basin with water for washing for every five children. Adult to child ratio for staffing should be one to eight, or one to ten if the adult is qualified. Furthermore equipment will be examined for condition, as well as the premises themselves. Questions must be answered about feeding provision and the keeping of records.

[1] This is the present (1970) legal position, but may change later. Some education authorities are already taking an active interest in play groups.

The interpretation of the requirements is the responsibility of the Medical Officer, but clearly it is desirable to get as close to conforming with the requirements as is physically possible in the local circumstances.

The cost of starting a group will be the responsibility of a local committee which will raise the money needed in the usual way. There are however possibilities of grants from various sources and the National Association of Pre-School Play groups should be contacted about these (see below). In most areas free milk is available for the children, paid for, and then reclaimed. For this a form must be completed (obtainable from Health Visitor or M.O.H.) and returned to the Ministry of Health, Saville Row, London, W.1. Frequently the Public Health Department will also be able to help with second-hand nursery equipment.

The staffing of the group is of very first importance, and the person who is to be in charge must be found before the group is formed. It is no use beginning on a casual *ad hoc* basis. If possible the leader or supervisor should be a trained Nursery School teacher or Nursery nurse. Married teachers or nurses with young children of their own are an obvious choice. In their absence a suitable mother can run a group, but continuity of responsibility is essential both for the children and for the other mothers who may be asked to assist on a rota basis. What the supervisor or helpers should be paid is a matter for personal arrangement. Decisions about charges to be made, how many sessions to run a week, how many children to accept, will all be dependent upon local resources.

Two points are of particular importance, both of which will be mentioned in rather more detail in the appropriate chapters. First the pastor will be aware of areas of particular social or environmental need in his parish. Such areas are a first call upon play group places. It is of course true that all children need what the group has to offer, but most will make up for play deficiency in the facilities they will later receive at school. Some however may be so severely deprived of space, play materials, chances for self-expression and social contact, that irreparable damage is done which even the most favourable schooling after five years of age will not compensate. Schools in areas of severe deprivation tend themselves to suffer many of the defects of their area—over-crowding, restricted play space, staff changes, and so on. The provision of play groups in such areas is of tremendous importance and should be given priority over provision else-where. This may be a hard saying and more fortunately situated parent groups may wax very vocal in their assertion that they have every right to serve their own children. But in the context of any discussion of the pastoral ministry priorities must be asserted unequivocally.

The second point concerns the needs of individual children. These are of course often difficult to discover or ascertain. However statutory social agencies in every authority are in touch with such children and their families. Every play group should hold a certain number of places vacant and free for children referred to them from Child Guidance Clinics, Children's Departments, or other agencies. When children are sent to fill these places they may present difficulties. In some cases supervisors may find that they attend for a few sessions and then disappear. There would be great value in the appointment to each play group of someone who was prepared to follow up each referred child, first with the agency that sent him and then with the child's home. The object of such follow-up would be to ensure that the play group had done all it could to meet the child's and the parents' problems. Transport, lack of suitable clothing, mothers' absence somewhere for periods which made it impossible to deliver and collect her child, are a few reasons for absence and ones which the play group should be able to meet.

MEETING COMMUNITY NEEDS
OF THE UNDER FIVES

Enough has been said above to indicate ways in which the pre-school child may be cared for outside his home assuming "normal" conditions within it. However conditions are not always normal. In some circumstances families are rendered particularly vulnerable by circumstances beyond their control. Such families have a particular call upon the pastoral care of the church and the community.

Simon Yudkin, before his tragic death in 1967, published a pamphlet *o–5: A Report on the Care of Pre-school Children.* He cited many of the anomalies at present existing within the administration of the Health and Education services of the country and pressed for a Government enquiry to clear these up. In so doing he drew attention to seven groups of families which particularly need attention. These seven groups might well be taken by every pastor as the points of special need within any community. They are a starting point for parochial policy which seeks out need and devises ways of meeting it or of cooperating with other services in this task. The seven groups are as follows:

(*a*) Unsupported families, i.e. when there is only one parent (unmarried mothers and families where the parents are separated or divorced, or where one parent has died or has deserted the family or is in prison, mother or father being in sole charge of the children).

(*b*) Families where father is ill or disabled or for other reasons is unable to act as the breadwinner.

(*c*) Families where the mother is mentally or physically unable to care for her home and the children.

(*d*) Physically or mentally handicapped children living at home.

(*e*) Families when mother as well as father goes out to work full time or part time.

(*f*) Families where there are several children of pre-school age.

(*g*) Families living in accommodation which is so restricted that the young child's normal development may be impaired.

There are no doubt many sincere Christians who feel that such groups within the community have, or ought to have,

all the attention that is needed from the welfare agencies.
Dr Yudkin made it abundantly clear that they are not in
fact getting this help to the extent that is required. This
leaves two approaches from the Church wide open and demanding help. Every pastor will make it his business to
know those who are responsible for welfare provision in his
community (see Chapter 6). From them and from others he
will soon learn the gaps in such provision and do what he
can through his lay people to fill them. But this still leaves
the one essential pastoral role which he will recognize,
namely the pastoral care and befriending of those who stand
most in need of it. Here he will find the greatest drain upon
his own personal resources of faith, patience, courage, and
love of people for Christ's sake. Here he will find a role
which is peculiarly his own but which he will share with his
lay colleagues because the demands will be too great for him
alone.

In his ministry to the under fives the pastor will be serving
the most impressionable and the most vulnerable members
of his community. He is well advised to seek every possible
help and cooperation that he can secure, as well as offering
himself and his parochial resources openly to all involved
in this task.

4

Children Learning

Anyone over thirty years of age who has visited the infant and junior department of a modern primary school will be aware that the methods of helping children to learn have undergone very distinctive changes in the last twenty years. These changes relate not only to the materials which are used in the classroom, but also to the whole attitude to learning expressed both by teachers and children. The classroom atmosphere has changed from a formal and disciplined situation to one that, to the uninitiated, looks like chaos. The seating arrangements no longer suggest a frontal encounter between teacher and taught, but rather a co-operative activity in which small groups of children engage upon a joint task and the teacher assumes a peripatetic and helpful role rather than an authoritarian and didactic one. Different groups of children are doing different things; there is an abundance of material available to them, some of it unrecognizable to one whose education was completed before 1940; indeed, for many taught in less progressive or financially restricted schools, before 1960. What underlies these very radical changes?

In the post-war years a great deal of attention has been given to the psychology of learning, not only how children learn but also learning in animals. The modern technological world demands more and more "educated" persons to run it, and education in this sense means not culture but adaptability and creativity. Throughout every branch of education, from the infant classroom to the most elaborate training centres for adult technicians, there is an almost frantic search for ways of teaching and learning that will secure the optimum results from every pupil in the shortest possible time. Around this search for efficiency and expertise a gigantic educational industry has developed in which places of further education and technical experts combine to produce professional experts in every branch of human activity.

From a critical standpoint much of what passes for education may fall far short of the definition that the purist might give to the word. Student protest in recent years has quite unequivocally shown that not all those being taught consider that they are being educated, but this is a philosophical question about which a few suggestions will be made in the next chapter. The purpose of this chapter is to outline briefly some of the reasons for the sort of change referred to in the first paragraph and to suggest ways in which we may broaden our conception of the word "education".

THEORIES OF LEARNING

For the psychologist who is studying how learning takes place, learning must be defined in terms of doing since, if nothing is done, there is nothing that can be measured. It is through changes in activity brought about by changes in the situation of the learner that learning can be studied.

Theories of learning are essentially theories, that is, different ways of describing what are the generally accepted facts and what happens. Different theories are not therefore mutually exclusive; one often contains or develops another or explains a process with which the other is not concerned. Theories tend to fall into three broad groups:

1. Theories based upon Stimulus and Response, and which for the most part result from the observation of experiments with animals in a laboratory situation.
2. Cognitive theories, i.e. theories based upon a study of how people think.
3. Theories resulting from the observation of children's behaviour at different stages of development. Such theories

are known as developmental and are commonly associated with the name of the Swiss psychologist, Jean Piaget.

We will discuss the first two quite briefly and the third in rather more detail.

Stimulus–Response theories and all their subsequent modifications began with the famous experiment of Pavlov with his dog. Pavlov noticed that the presence of food caused increase in salivation. If a bell was rung a second or two before food was offered, the association of the sound and the food could result in salivation at the sound only. In this experiment the bell is the stimulus, salivation is the response, and the food is what is called a reinforcer. It is the reinforcer which is the essential link between S and R. Transformed into the schoolroom situation this process of "operant conditioning", as it is called, appears in simple programmed learning. A programme presents a simple problem (complex problems being broken down into simple ones), the child presents the answer (selects the right button or writes in a blank space provided), and the machine reinforces his finding either by showing a green light or allowing him to move to the next problem. Such a method is, of course, clearly helpful in learning-situations which have a right and a wrong answer. Many situations, however, are neutral and do not possess a single answer. This has led to elaborate programme systems known as "branching". In many cases problems of this sort are better dealt with by cognitive methods.

Cognitive theories of learning have their origin in much the same type of experiment as S–R theories but take a broader view of the processes involved in problem solving. The word most closely associated with these theories is "gestalt". A *"Gestalt"* is a set of circumstances which constitute a unit and in which change in one circumstance brings about change in all the others. Learning consists of "seeing" or "thinking out" the significance of all the parts of the unit in order to arrive at the solution of the problem. The expression "insightful learning" has been applied to this process. Insight takes advantage of previous learning, as well as the immediate circumstances. Response is now to a broad range of factors past and present rather than to a single presented stimulus. It is the ability to organize knowledge that makes learning possible. This certainly appears to be a more satisfactory theory when applied to human learning than the seemingly very mechanical process of S–R. But the valuable contribution of S–R must not be passed over. It is from S–R that present day techniques of advanced programmed learning have been evolved. The understanding of the nature of reinforcers and their association with the stimulus overlaps into many learning situations. Word and image association are often used in the psychological testing of children. The observation of scientifically demonstrable facts about behaviour is a healthy balancer to the theoretical complexities of psychoanalysis.

JEAN PIAGET AND
DEVELOPMENT PSYCHOLOGY

In the last decade much attention has been given by educationists to the developmental psychology of Professor Jean Piaget who has devoted much time to the study of child development and particularly to learning development. The theories he has elaborated have appeared over a long period beginning in the 1930s and still continuing. But it is comparatively recently that his work has been recognized in educational circles in this country, and only in the last decade that an effort has been made to apply his findings in the general field of religious education.

Piaget is not an easy author to read though, once made, the effort is rewarding. There are, however, a number of useful summaries of his work for the benefit of those who have not the time to tackle the originals.

Piaget sees development as a dynamic process in the course of which the child becomes increasingly able to adjust to and control his environment. In explaining this process he uses two words which are important for his whole thought, namely, *assimilation* and *accommodation*. The understanding of these words may be helped by an analogy with the biological sciences. Assimilation may be compared with the "taking in" by living organisms of substances—food oxygen, etc., from the environment in order to sustain the life and promote the growth of the organism. So the child assimilates the elements of his food which his body needs and rejects the waste material. The extent of health and growth depends upon what the environment offers and thus changes in response to his assimilation of the environment. But the nature of the change is conditional upon the resources of the environment to which he accommodates himself as best he can. This process of assimilation and accommodation goes on continuously. When what is taken in is adequate a state of equilibrium between assimilation and accommodation is reached; but if it is inadequate the child or other organism will seek compensation in order to produce equilibrium. But even when all is well and the environment is producing the necessary means of life and growth, this very fact increases the child's demands upon the environmental resources. So equilibrium once reached is never stable for very long. Growth towards maturity enables the child not only to increase his demands but also to control and manipulate his environment for his own ends.

This analogy can now be transferred to the development of the child's thinking processes to help us understand what Piaget is saying. Take two quite simple examples the first in which accommodation is difficult and secondly one in which it is achieved. A five-year-old child is given a toy car which needs winding to make it run along. He is shown the way it is done, but the adult does not perhaps realize that the child's manipulative ability is not up to the skill and strength required to turn the winding key. Left to himself the child will try and fail; he will accommodate to the situation by using the toy in the way past experience has suggested, namely as a push-along model; but this does not work either—it won't push. Frustrated he may break it or discard it. However much he may wish to achieve a certain result he must accept his own limitations and the intractability of objects. Later his increasing experience and ability to transfer or adapt experience of one situation to another will help him to solve his problems in a more satisfactory way—for example, at six and a half Simon winds a motor by putting the flat of the winder in a gap between floor boards and turning the motor. Observation of children's modes of accommodation are an important guide to ways in which they are thinking and the stages they have reached.

More positive examples of accommodation may often be seen with four to six-year-olds at play. The adult world is a very intractable one in which the child's role is often a battle against the forces of adult "good order and discipline"; in the course of the struggle the child has to cope with frustration, disappointment, and apparent and real misunderstanding by adults of his needs and desires. Unable to control reality to meet his needs he uses toys and other objects to hand as symbols of his intractable environment. Thus reduced to manageable symbols, reality can be manipulated and accommodated and some degree of equilibrium achieved. A toy car and roadway of bricks may easily be a returning parent whose absence is felt with some degree of anxiety. A plastic duck thrown out of a group of toys can be someone whose presence is an irritant—someone taking up parental attention—sibling or other adult.

Piaget finds three major stages in a child's development. Each of these subdivides into further stages, but for our purposes a glance at the three main ones will have to be sufficient. These are:

1. The sensori-motor stage which covers the period from birth to eighteen months.
2. The stage of concrete operations which extends from eighteen months to eleven years.
3. The stage of formal operations which reaches its apogee at about fifteen years.

Stage One. At birth and through the first month an infant is capable of little more than reflex actions. Gradually he comes to enjoy certain actions and repeats them intentionally. By nine months or so he is already on the way to performing certain patterns of behaviour in order to achieve certain ends. He will at this stage discover that objects such as his rattle or toy are permanent though not necessarily visible; hide the rattle under the blanket and he will look for it where he has seen it hidden; hide it in a *new place* and he will, in spite of having seen it hidden, first look in the original hiding place, but by about one year will go straight to the new one. It has become permanent even when "displaced", i.e. put in another position in space. By one and a half he has advanced a long way; he can find an object hidden behind an obstruction by going round the obstruction. He can make detours and return to his starting point by the same route. He will use past experience to solve new problems; for example, if he has discovered that the point of a pencil will fit a hole, he will turn a pencil presented blunt end forward so that he has the point available to make the fit. He is, however, working on past experience; he cannot yet relate the size or shape of the hole to the point of the pencil. He must wait a little while yet before the "posting shapes" type of toy can be used by any other method than trial and error.

Along with the ability to interiorize actions, i.e. to think them through rather than act out each stage, comes the beginning of language. These two factors of development lay the foundations for the next stage.

Stage Two is a long one and is given several subdivisions, but for our purposes we can distinguish two, namely, a stage which marks the development of representational or symbolic thinking and a further stage of concrete operations in which the child will learn to handle relationships between objects but not relationships between relationships. This means that he can handle observations at the concrete level and make first stage deductions from what he has observed. But he cannot yet compare deductions and arrive at a proposition dependent upon them.

The period of symbolic thinking is well demonstrated in

the child's play. What appears to be simple imitation is, in fact, the way in which reality is seen and integrated in order that it may be dealt with as we have seen above. Speaking of a child's imitative games Piaget says, "In a word they form a vast network of devices which allow the ego to assimilate the whole of reality, i.e. integrate it in order to relive it, to dominate it in order to compensate for it." Up to the age of about four and a half the child is still very much dependent upon concrete experience. Each experience and each activity is particular, a part of a learned schema; there is as yet no consistent deductive reasoning. Language is developing and verbal commands are understood, but often overlaid by motor actions which cannot fully be controlled. It is the last and most powerful stimulus that will determine response. He is not yet capable of putting things in order, either mentally or physically, with any degree of consistency and will explain a thing in one way at one moment and in another, even contradictory, way a moment later.

The second subdivision of this second stage is the most adventurous and exciting period of childhood both for children and parents. Around the age of five just as school begins, a state of reasonable equilibrium will have been achieved by symbolic play and language as we have seen. But like all such equilibria it is immediately disturbed by its own potentialities. Now begins a period of lively and intensive exploration of the environment. This exploration makes heavy demands on teachers and parents but is an essential part of the whole learning process. This period is appropriately called that of "concrete operations" because it is the concrete world around him that the child is striving to master. The name is also appropriate because the limitation to which the child has to accommodate is precisely concrete as opposed to abstract thinking. We have seen that at four years of age in fitting the point of pencil into a hole he works on the basis of experience alone. Now between the ages of five and seven we can watch the way in which he will begin to discover relationships between objects. The test situations for this stage of development have now become classic and are cited in most accounts of Piaget's work. We will take two of these.

A box of wooden beads is shown to a group of five to seven-year-olds. Some of the beads are white, but most are brown. The children are shown that all are wooden. They are asked "Are there more brown beads or more wooden beads?" The children find this difficult to answer, because they are confused by the two categories of colour and substance being presented simultaneously. The whole (wooden) and the parts making up the whole (white and brown) cannot be related to one another. But the older children of the group will probably, after some thought, arrive at the correct answer and the reason for it. The same experiment with eight-year-olds will produce the right answer at once.

A set of wooden rods of different lengths is put in front of the same group and the children are told to arrange them in order of size. The younger children will do this unsystematically by comparing pairs. The older members of the group will soon arrange them correctly working systematically.

Thus by about seven there is recognition of relationships between objects and an ability to arrange objects or to break down a group of objects into classes according to the relationships between them.

Further experiments with children between seven and eleven will reveal how gradually there develops an understanding of the permanence or conservation of substance (learned first and quite early on in stage one), then of volume, and finally of weight. But in all the experiments the learning process is confined to the concrete situation or problem with which the child is faced. Only at the end of this stage does he begin to form concepts from his experiences which he will apply in a variety of different situations or in symbolic language without the concrete objects in front of him.

Stage Three. The third stage in the development of children's thinking begins at about eleven and coincides with adolescence. In the previous stage of concrete operations the child has made a number of discoveries about things and events. He has learned to classify, to arrange series and so on; now he begins to derive propositions from his discoveries which he is able to consider apart from the concrete situation in which they arose. The concepts so formed are now freed from their object sources and can be related to one another. This is what may be described as "second-stage" grouping.

The significant advance in this stage of formal operations lies in the ability of the child to abstract and reapply the principle which he has abstracted in another and different situation. This sort of thinking is essential to progress in science, which concerns the application of laws or experimental findings in different situations and with different substances. It is also essential in any subject which has an abstract vocabulary and demands abstract thinking. The language of religion and the religious thinking are highly abstract. It is this fact that has raised so much questioning in the minds of teachers about the suitability for young children of much Christian doctrinal teaching.

Piaget's developmental psychology has not been accepted without criticism. There have been rather technical criticisms relating to his research methods and his rather unsophisticated methods of analysing his observations. In general subsequent investigations based upon his findings have born out the main contentions of his scheme but modified details. The most telling criticism which demands further research is scarcely a criticism of Piaget himself but of the environment in which he worked. The children whom he observed were either his own or other Swiss children who were being educated in the formal methods characteristic of the years between 1920 and 1940. How typical are such children of those of today who have a much more permissive upbringing with opportunity for experience and discovery from the infant class onwards? It might well be that in a favourable environment, with improved teaching techniques, the ages at which different stages of development are reached might have to be substantially revised. Furthermore the Swiss children of Piaget's writings are not typical of the slow learning child from a poor environment whose developmental progress is often much slower than Piaget suggests. This is well summed up by Molly Brearley:

> A difficulty of interpretation has arisen by a too literal gearing of ages and stages. Piaget gives the average ages for the attainment of the stages of thinking of the children he tested. He is less concerned with this, however, than with the order of the stages and the mastery of the material within them, which he claims is constant.
>
> He does not look on these as maturational levels or as educational ones but as the result of assimilation and accommodation which in their turn are dependent on the interaction between maturation and experience.[1]

The implications of Piaget's work or, for that matter, the work of the many psychologists and educationists who have added to our knowledge of how children learn, will be discussed in the next chapter.

[1] *A Teacher's Guide to Reading Piaget*, p. 169.

Home and School

At present, and most probably for some time to come, the Church is involved in education at all levels. By the Act of 1944 religious education was made a compulsory subject in all schools. As a result of past history the Church has a number of schools and colleges of education which are an integral part of the educational system of the country. Within the church school instruction is given in the teach-ings of the Church of England. In all schools a daily act of worship is a compulsory part of the curriculum.

So long as future Education Acts demand or even permit inclusion of Religious Education in the school curriculum, the Church has not only a responsibility but an opportunity to minister to children in a quite unique way. No Christian today supposes that religious studies surpass any other department of knowledge in importance or should dominate an education curriculum, but all Christians know that the child who has no knowledge of the religious approach to life lacks an essential means of interpreting himself and his world. The vision of himself and of his fellow men which is opened to the child by the Christian gospel is not replace-able by any other subject that he may be taught. The religious provisions of the Act of 1944 gave the Churches an opportunity to share this vision with all children regard-less of their background, ability, or denomination.

In so far as church schools are a part of the national educational endeavour there can be no question of dual standards. Church schools must be, and be seen to be, as efficient, up-to-date, and well staffed as any other school within the system. No child entering a church school shall, as a result of his parents' option, if this has been exercised, or of his residence in the school's catchment area, suffer any disadvantage from the Church's management of the school. It is not sufficient to provide religious training of a thorough and effective sort at the expense of education in other parts of the curriculum. Whether the school is aided or controlled it is first and foremost the place for the total education of the children who attend, and any bias which results in undue emphasis of the Church's role will reflect upon its educational efficiency.

What then is religious education? Do we not in fact possess these schools for the very purpose of providing this bias? Is not this just what the parents of the children are asking for when they enter the children for a church school? This is arguable. Some parents may indeed expect such a bias, though it is unfortunate if they actually want it rather than a well-balanced curriculum.

The religious education of children is not a matter of giving exclusive attention to doctrinal instruction and the practice of Christian worship; it is the whole education of the child in such a manner that his spiritual needs and aspirations are given an opportunity to develop alongside all other facets of his growth to which equal attention must be given. It is important that every child shall have the opportunity of recognizing the existence of a spiritual interpretation of his world and of his place and role within it. But how does it come about that any such interpretation is made possible?

> Religious Education always starts from membership of a group which has a religious outlook, even if the group consists of only two people: a parent and his child, a teacher—whether he be a specialist or a form master—and a pupil.[1]

The direction the child's interpretation of life will take depends upon the relationships he forms at home and at school. It is also of course dependent upon his developmental stage and the nature of his experience. None of these

[1] W. R. Niblett. *Education and the Modern Mind*. Faber 1967

factors can be seen in isolation. But the situation demanded by Professor Niblett as a necessary context of communication underlies all of them. Whatever methods may be employed, however well informed, the child remains religiously uneducated unless the spark of personal conviction and attitude is communicated by another human being. But this does not mean that the classroom is a suitable place for evangelism.

THE CHILD AND THE HOME

We have understood enough about the growing child from the previous chapters to recognize the determining role of parent-child relationships. But we have not faced the question of what is the religious context, if any, of this relationship; or where, within it, religion is communicated. To the religious all life is religious; therefore in general terms we may say that the communication is in fact an ongoing process which is so linked to the development of the growing person that it is indistinguishable from it. Nevertheless the question of verbal expression of the religious nature of life must be faced. When and on what occasions do we use the word God? It is no use avoiding this issue, since from at least the age of five onwards the word, the language, and story associated with it will be familiar to the child in various contexts outside the home. Unless some positive attitude is taken by parents the meanings attached to them may be confusing and misleading.

We have learned from the previous chapter that the intellectual development of the child makes it impossible for him to grasp abstract concepts with any real degree of understanding much before the age of twelve. We have also seen how thinking is limited in the middle period of childhood to the concrete situation, the experienced reality. Any attempt that we make to answer questions about God, of which the child will produce several from an early age, will lead us into all sorts of abstractions which will be meaningless, or concrete explanations which are likely to sow more seeds of subsequent confusion than produce helpful answers to the questions. The most satisfactory replies to these questions must be in the context of his own life in association with the life of Jesus or of those who are signal examples of his teaching. God can only be knowable to the young child in terms of his own experience or possibly in terms of the experiences of others which, when adequately told, afford some scope for personal identification.

In this process of helping the child to interpret his world in religious terms his own experiences are absolutely paramount. These experiences will be of two sorts, not always easily separable. First, there are what we can term maturational experiences. These spring from within the child and result from the stage of growth that he has reached. For example, the infant of six months separated for even a short time (two or three days) from his mother will show signs of anxiety which will not be present in his three-year-old brother; the six-year-old playing a game with rules expects his adult opponent to keep the rules, but will fly into a temper if the adult imposes the rules on him; the ten-year-old however will religiously keep the rules himself and expect his opponent to do the same; any suggestion of waiving the rules for any reason will "spoil the game". Feelings of dependence, aggression, egocentricism, role identification, the oedipal affiliations, growing sexual awareness, self-consciousness in early adolescence are all maturational experiences of great intensity. Often these are not appreciated and a young child will suffer the judgement of an adult who can only think in terms of adult behaviour. A six-year-old child will be accused of lying when in fact he is still unable to sort out reality and fantasy or command the vocabulary suitable for a "true" explanation.

The second sort of experience consists of the shape taken by the environment around the child—the physical, intellectual, and emotional atmosphere of home, school, and community, the things he plays with, the places he is taken to, the language he hears, the stories he is read. These may be wide in range or they may be restricted. They will have a very substantial influence upon his learning and his personality development.

The purpose of education in the full sense of the word is to ensure that the environment of the child facilitates the growth and maturation of the personality by relating these two sorts of experience. Thus strong feelings of aggression in young children need the means of expression in permissible form; adult understanding which will ensure that aggression is not met with aggression nor with a response calculated to generate guilt.

It is in this educational process of adult response to the child's needs that religious education is really conducted. Experience of love, forgiveness, sympathy, tolerance, stability, dependability will slowly put together an understanding of God. Without these God will remain an unintelligible cypher. How, and how often, parents and teachers will choose to make verbally explicit the revelation of God in experience is a matter for study beyond what can be dealt with here. But there are occasions in the child's life and in the lives of those around him that offer such opportunities. They must be taken with care and, above all, with a knowledge of the child which should be but often is not possessed by parents. It is here that the pastor's role is essential. All that can conceivably be done to help busy parents become sensitive to their children's needs will be an addition to the pastoral ministry to the child.

But this adult response to need does not take place in the home only. It spills over into the community; it is part of the Church's work with children wherever the Church is in touch with them—club, Sunday school, holiday camp, in the street, in the church. In this delicate and critical matter of interpretation no pastor can be satisfied with the lowest common factor in terms of adult help. There must be trained and mature adults who not only understand the children but have so struggled and continue to struggle towards a deepening of their own faith that they are able to communicate to the children what their own experience has taught them to be significant.

The pastoral care and education of the child is thus inseparable from the care and education of the adult. This reinforces what has been said above about the inseparability of child and home in all our thinking about the ministry to him. As he grows so we must constantly be aware of his extending environment and our need to see ministry as a wide complex of interrelated parts.

THE PASTOR AS INTERPRETER
BETWEEN HOME AND SCHOOL

Our discussion in Chapter 3 of the insights gained in recent years into children's learning showed that the gap between the education of parents and the education of their children is a very wide one. Curriculum teaching methods, the physical lay-out of the classroom, and the outside school activities of children during the school day all raise questions in the parents' minds about the effectiveness and value of the teaching their children are receiving. Few parents understand the new maths; many are impatient when faced with the practical implications of "reading readiness"; many cannot understand what the children are doing visiting a farm or factory, or running around the town with note-books and little apparent purpose. Anxiety and criticism are understandable, but they can also be damaging to the child's educational development. The support of the parents has a marked effect upon the performance of the children. Parents cannot offer adequate support of methods they do not understand.

In recent years Parent-Teacher associations have done much to awaken in parents a desire to understand what their own children are doing at school and so be of more help to them at home. Through such associations teachers have learnt to appreciate the value of a personal knowledge and understanding of their children's homes. The involvement in and encouragement of such associations is an essential part of the pastor's work with children. Where they do not exist the initiation of some common meeting ground between parents and teachers will be valued by both sides.

But this role of interpreter is not just to be exercised in relation to the school. The methods used in school are also being used out of school. Voluntary children's work, from the infants in Sunday schools to confirmation and post-confirmation training, is assuming a radically new look. What is being done is based largely upon the same educational principles that are guiding school work. These principles, some of which we have discussed in Chapter 3, have demanded a fresh examination of the applicability to children of much of the doctrinal content of our teaching. So educational method and theological reappraisal have produced as disturbing a situation for parents in the religious upbringing of their children as have the changed methods in the schools. Interpretation in this situation is something which no pastor can avoid. If lack of parental support can be damaging to a child's school performance, how much more damaging can it be to his chances of religious growth and development.

It is easy to say that the pastor must interpret, but he cannot begin this task until he is himself sure of the language he is required to translate. For a very long time the training of parochial clergy before or after ordination in any real educational understanding has been lamentably neglected. Efforts have been made and are increasingly being made to close this breach in pastoral training. But it will have to be taken very much more seriously if it is to be effective.

WAYS OF INTERPRETATION

In recent years schools have begun seriously to tackle the problem of interpretation and there is a growing literature on the relationship of school and home. In some places verbal explanations at parents' meetings or open days have been replaced by classes for parents in which they have been subjected to the same methods as their children. Parents have found themselves learning how to use cuisinère rods and Dienes apparatus, have had a go at using the science apparatus associated with Nuffield courses, have sat at a desk in a language laboratory, have had a skilled teacher explain in detail a project laid out in front of them in a classroom and understood the part their own child has played in it. These experiences have produced understanding and enthusiasm and have opened up ways in which parents can assist the educational process by providing the right sort of experiences at home.

In his parochial work there are many activities in connection with the children through which the pastor will seek to deepen the children's understanding of the gospel and inform their worship and broaden their knowledge. The purpose of many of these activities may not be easily understood by parents. Following the examples of the schools the pastor should take every opportunity to do with parent groups very much what he has done with the children.

Experiments with the training of clergy and voluntary teachers for work with children has shown that real understanding of method comes about when, like small children, they get on the floor with paper, scissors and paste and do the job themselves.

This is so not only at the simpler levels of creative and experiential learning but also at the deeper level of worship. Adults are more inhibited than children, more inclined to shelter behind formularies that do not offer too close a personal identification or are pleasantly nostalgic without having any particular meaning for them. But, if persuaded to exercise a free hand in devising worship which arises from an immediate and shared experience, they soon detect the value of relevance, simplicity of expression, diversity of ways of expression, the use of words which have a meaning for them—the cry to God which is an intelligible issue from their own condition. All these are the things which the pastor seeks to do with his children and can do with parents in such a way that the two are brought closer together. Simple explanation can accompany such activities, but it should remain simple. The real point is—This is how your children are working and worshipping.

If the session has been effective the point will go home without much additional verbal emphasis.

THE PASTOR AND THE SCHOOL

The relationship of the pastor to the school in his parish is governed by law (see Appendix I) and by the relationship established with the headmaster. Friction between parochial clergy and school staff should be avoided at all costs since any work which is done in school will depend upon cooperation and understanding one another's roles. Although a member of the parish staff or the incumbent may possess an educational qualification, this does not imply that he is therefore more skilled in teaching religion in school than the headmaster. The school is the headmaster's responsibility just as the church is the incumbent's, and the autonomy of each within his own sphere must be recognized. It is the professional role of each that needs to be understood and respected. These roles are assumed not only on the basis of qualification but also on the position each occupies in the community; the community's expectation of function, although often very different from the professional's self view, must be taken seriously if interpretation is to be effective. If this is clear then the way is open for much very profitable cooperation.

There are three ways in which a pastoral ministry may be exercised in the school—school worship, class teaching, and pastoral concern for the staff. There are other ways, but most fall within these three headings.

SCHOOL WORSHIP

An act of worship is a compulsory part of the school day. It will frequently happen that an invitation to take this or to take part in it will be extended to local clergy. If it is a church school it will of course be an ongoing part of the work of the parochial clergy.

School assembly presents more problems than any other part of the religious activity of the school. In spite of a substantial number of books providing material for school worship, little real progress has been made in devising a mode of worship which is acceptable to the children and physically possible in the conditions in which it has to take place. The act demands (at present) that the day shall *begin* with an act of worship. Many teachers feel that it would be more appropriate if it ended with one, or, if this presents difficulties, that each class should have its own act of worship at whatever time is appropriate. It is hoped that this sort of flexibility may be possible in the future; indeed it is already the practice in many schools.

In devising an act of worship the three principles mentioned above—participation, relevance, and intelligibility —should be the guide-lines. The temptation to teach or moralize in worship should be avoided and the content should speak to the children's condition and experience. A knowledge of the children's background, home, and community experience is essential if relevance is to be assured. Opportunity should be taken to elicit from the children the matters which are of immediate concern to them, individually and collectively, and these should form the varying and ongoing content. From time to time children, even young children, should be encouraged to use their newspapers and television to broaden their area of concern, in worship, to the community and world in which they live. Momentous events will be easy, but smaller details and insights will need the guidance of the teacher or pastor. The use of readings from or about notable people past or present is common in many books of forms of service for assembly. Though well known and seemingly significant for the adult such "exempla" tend to be irrelevant to the children, reflecting situations in which they do not find themselves. Worship may well arise from a well done project about a specific subject or personality, or from a well written and emotive account of an event, but the short reading unbacked by prior knowledge and understanding is unlikely to provoke in children the sort of response that worship demands.[1]

[1] See Chapter 10 for further and more devoted treatment.

CLASS TEACHING

Every minister is, to some extent, a teacher. This is true in his work with adults as well as with children. But there are many interpretations of the word "teach" and only some of these refer to the classroom activity. No minister should feel that, because he doesn't have either the ability or the inclination for classroom teaching, he has therefore no ability to minister to children. He may well have other and far more important gifts to communicate. This doesn't mean that he should not visit the school but rather that his work in it may be better done in the staff room or the playground than in the classroom.

In previous chapters we have tried to indicate some of the ways in which children learn. The need to relate the subject matter that is being taught to the capacity of the children to deal with it goes without saying. The main problem that faces the pastor in the classroom is the tension between straight, non-sectarian teaching and the desire to evangelize. It has been said above that the classroom is not the appropriate place for evangelism. It is also true that the parish priest in the classroom will undoubtedly be assumed to be occupying the same role as in the parish—at least if the school in which he is teaching is in the parish. This tension has to be met. It is much easier to meet if the minister has an educational qualification which will enable him to enter the school on the same footing as the rest of the staff. In this case he will fit in with whatever syllabus or method is being followed in the school and will make his contribution by exercising his dual role of educationist and theologian. If he is unqualified he must be what he is and what the children expect him to be—the local minister who will be able to talk about the religious life of the community and the work and worship of his church, answer their questions and clarify their understanding of the Christian faith. Though possibly more limited in the ground he can cover from the school's point of view, he can, on grounds of relevance and informality which the children will appreciate, offer the school something which no other member of staff can contribute. Since the unqualified minister is unlikely to be invited to take a class except at the occasional invitation of the headmaster, his appearance will be an "event" and an acceptable break in routine. Every care should be taken to see that it comes up to the children's expectations.

RELIGIOUS EDUCATION
AND THE CHURCH SCHOOL

Although the church school might seem the most obvious focus for evangelism within the parish, to treat it in this way will endanger its main purpose, which is a total education into which religious education is integrated; but since it is a denominational school it will offer the opportunity of participation in the life of the local Christian community. This will have its own evangelical results. Class teaching however must remain teaching, not preaching. The Church's participation in education and its community life are complementary activities which should not be allowed to become confused. The school is the place in which the child may expect to receive a good groundwork of knowledge and understanding of Christian teaching, history, and modern practice which will give reason and meaning to Church life and practice within the community. For these reasons Christian teaching in the church school should be of the highest possible quality and should employ the most up-to-date and efficient methods of communication.

Once this sort of efficiency is achieved the way is open for the voluntary work of the Church to concentrate upon the caring work which is its responsibility, and upon the relational aspects of Christian growth which lie at the root of true *koinonia*. It is unfortunate that much of the voluntary work with children has to take the form of an often inefficient and only semi-skilled version of what should be taking place in school. These complementary roles may not be easy to achieve but at least they should form the criteria of pastoral policy. This is not to suggest that the church school should be restricted to the less exciting and more formal role of communicating information, but rather should ensure that whatever else is done this role is fulfilled as adequately as possible. By the use of modern methods of communication, project work, individual research, and community studies, the necessary factual background of knowledge can be built up without the need to resort to unacceptable formal methods. There is an increasing range of material becoming available for the teacher, and new methods of approach are increasing the flexibility of the subject. Community studies and community service provide an approach which makes it possible to integrate religious studies with other parts of the curriculum and ensure maximum participation at all levels of ability. At the same time the range of material available for the communication of information enables this part of the syllabus to have a broad curricular basis and stimulate a wide range of interest. It is this broad and flexible approach to the religious education of the child which will prepare the way for a general attitude throughout the life of the school in which Christian values are communicated to the children in the normal course of their development.

An integrated curriculum once established in a school does of course mean that the flexibility offered to the children must be paralleled by a flexibility among the staff. If members of a parochial team are involved in the work of the school they must be aware of the regular time schedule which the school may demand of them and provision for this must be included in parochial planning. A single-handed minister may find this difficult, in which case he will probably be best employed in working with the staff in the planning of the activities rather than actually taking part in them.

THE PASTOR AND THE STAFF
OF THE SCHOOL

Concern for members of school staff will of course take its place in the normal pastoral care of all adults, but there are two particular points which should be noted. Enough has already been said to indicate the need for close association between minister and head teacher. What is sometimes not appreciated by the minister is the position of isolation in which he is often placed. This is particularly so in a community containing few schools. The head is frequently under conflicting pressures—managers and parents, parents and staff, children and staff. His decisions must be his own and the support of local authority officers or diocesan directors can only be occasionally invoked. The understanding and impartiality of the pastor and the comparability of their relative roles in the community can often be of great value to him and should always be available. In the case of church schools of course the responsibility is a shared one. The second point concerns the new and younger members of staff. Frequently a new member of staff may be only very recently out of college, removed often some considerable distance from home and from the home community or Christian congregation. In addition there are pressures within the school in both classroom and staff-room which may increase the sense of loneliness and inexperience. Though not always the case these are factors which should receive the pastor's careful attention. Lay members of the parish team will help in the discovery and meeting of these needs.

6

Children with Special Needs

HANDICAPPED CHILDREN

Sooner or later every minister will be faced with the need to exercise pastoral care for a handicapped child and his family; he will visit the home of such a child or the institution or school which cares for or educates him, or the hospital ward in which he is receiving treatment. In each instance he will need some knowledge of the child and his needs and of the problems he presents for parents and professional workers. He will also need to have some parochial policy which does not leave the discovery of such children to the chance of random visiting but makes some attempt to assess the extent of need within the parish and to find ways of meeting it. Unless there is such a policy it will be very easy for parochial resources to be used up by the demands made upon them before any policy is put forward. In this way those who have the greatest need of care may be overlooked in the effort to provide for those who, with a little help, can well care for themselves. This chapter cannot hope to supply the details of such a policy, but will attempt an outline of the main categories of handicap and indicate further sources of information and help.

Handicap in a young child inevitably produces strains and tensions within the home which need the support and understanding, not only of the pastor, but of the community in which the family lives. Care for such families therefore extends beyond the pastor himself. He will need to inform his lay people about various sorts of handicap in such a way that the whole community may be helped towards an attitude of sympathy and understanding instead of ineffectual sentiment or unreasonable prejudice.

The consideration of the pastoral needs of handicapped children has therefore to include both parent and child. It is often the former that needs the closer attention.

WHO ARE THE "HANDICAPPED" CHILDREN?

For administrative convenience, both professional and practical, handicapped children are divided by the education authorities into categories. For each of these categories special educational provision is made. The categories are: 1. The educationally subnormal. 2. Delicate. 3. Physically handicapped. 4. Maladjusted. 5. Epileptic. 6. Blind and partially sighted. 7. Deaf and partially hearing. These last two categories are really four since the needs of each group are quite distinct. In addition to these are children with speech defects, with special reading difficulties, autistic children, and the severely subnormal who, for the first time, are soon to be included as part of the administrative responsibility of the Department of Education and Science. The Act effecting this transfer passed Parliament in July 1970 and will begin to be implemented by local education authorities from the beginning of April 1971.

Although the above categories cover those children who, because of their handicap, need special education, it would be quite misleading to limit our view of "handicap" simply to these groups. The largest group is the educationally subnormal, but while this group can include as many as 10% of all school children, that is about one million children, only about 1·5% are in special schools. The rest are in ordinary schools, some receiving special attention, some having to do the best they can, frequently in a low stream— the anxiety of their headmaster, the despair of their teachers. Special education attracts some of the finest and most able teachers in the profession, but there are far too few of them and training facilities, either initial or in-service, are not sufficient to meet the demand.

The above remarks give the impression that handicap is

primarily an educational matter. This is not so, though the future of most handicapped children is determined very largely by the educational treatment that they receive. An intelligent child from a normal home background can still come out on top in spite of many inadequacies in his education, but a handicapped child cannot afford any further limitations being placed upon his development, and his schooling is of vital importance. In spite of this the combination of home and community is equally important.

There is a warning about homes which we should heed. It is too readily supposed that the "bad" home is one in which there are visible signs of inadequacy or neglect, but as one writer puts it:

> I have known homes which on the surface appeared satisfactory but where the children were desperately in need of help, although it may be difficult to prove parental neglect or failure to control. I know also of families miserably poor, below the poverty line, with few household goods, where there is a deep affection for the children and a unifying warmth.[1]

A glance at the list of handicaps that we have given will show that most fall into the area of physical disability, but two at least are the product of other factors than physical defect—these are educational subnormality and maladjustment; in both cases the environmental background of the child is so important that it may well be the determining factor for his personality and his future.

There is no space here to detail the causes of subnormality or maladjustment, nor are these causes always clear even to the experts. Educational subnormality is really a technical term applied to a small proportion among these children who need special help, and it is applied as a result of ascertainment or test and usually leads to the placement of the child in a special school. The term is however widely used to cover, as we have said above, some 10% of school children who show evidence of backwardness. The great

[1] Mrs D. Greenald, J.P., contributor to *Children in Trouble*, Conference Report. University of Leeds Institute of Education 1968

majority of such children are capable of considerable achievement but are prevented from gaining it by factors beyond their control. These include bad home conditions, bad neighbourhood conditions, lack of parental encouragement, a sense of failure and frustration resulting from inadequate teachers, and a loveless home. Maladjustment may often be the result of an aggravation of any one of these factors, or of several, so severe as to disrupt the child's emotional development. The umbrella term "deprivation", though originally limited in application to children deprived of maternal care for a prolonged period at an early age, is now used widely to describe "handicap" which results from the inadequacy of the human and physical surroundings in which a child is brought up. It is in this community and home care of the child that the Church's pastoral ministry can be most effective.

In the introduction to a recent book *The Special Child*, the author writes:

> The parents of these children are those whose fears did come true, who have to face the problem of accepting their handicapped child while mourning for their hoped-for normal child; a problem which starts with the birth of the child and which only too often is exacerbated by the reactions of everyone else with whom the parents become involved—a problem in which all too often they feel unsupported and rejected.[1]

THE PASTORAL CARE OF THE HANDICAPPED CHILD

THE SEVERELY SUBNORMAL CHILD

Handicap always imposes stress upon a family however courageously or capably the handicap is carried. Stress shows itself in a variety of ways and arises for several different reasons. There are however certain forms of stress which repeatedly show themselves in the presence of certain types of handicap. Severe mental subnormality poses a problem of *acceptance* which not every parent can solve. The social

[1] *The Special Child*, Barbara Furneaux. Pelican 1969

stigma felt to attach to this defect, the sense of guilt and injustice, the extreme physical fatigue that caring for the child can bring, all contribute to tension between love and rejection. The parents will often take refuge in retreat from social contact, or will sincerely refuse a diagnosis and make repeated attempts to find someone who will give a more acceptable answer to their questions.

I was telephoned one morning by an anxious and desperate parent. Her seven-year-old child had been attending a local school but the headmaster had now told her that he could not accept him any longer and felt that he should be transferred to a special school or a training centre for SSN children. As a result of medical advice and the recommendation of an educational psychologist a place was offered at a nearby newly-built residential training centre. The mother insisted to me that these people did not understand her child. He was just a little backward in reading and number and individual attention would solve all his problems. In spite of expert and very experienced professional counselling and great effort on the part of the local authority to explain the worthwhileness to her child of the residential place offered for him, she insisted upon consulting a school agency which eventually found a place in a private school some 120 miles from home. This mother could not accept an assessment of her child, however expert, which conflicted with her own or her husband's social and educational expectations of their child.

The ability to accept a child for what he is, completely disregarding what he might wish him to be, is not easy for any parent. To accept a child who is, for one reason or another, not acceptable to the social milieu in which the parents make their lives is even more difficult. Yet for the Christian it represents the very kernel of his concept of relationship with other human beings. God's complete acceptance of each one of us signified in our baptism and our taking the sacrament of Christ's body is a starting-point and a continuing foundation for our struggle to accept others. Here lies the pastoral approach to the problem that faces the family with a handicapped child. (See above, "Angela's baptism", pp. 16–17.

It is noticeable that an experiment in holding "once a year" services for severely subnormal children and their parents in selected parish churches of one region resulted in a response which exceeded all expectation and has continued annually now for five years. Those of us who have been involved in these services have been conscious of the relief and pleasure, found and expressed by parents and friends of the children, at being in an atmosphere of complete acceptance of the children as God's children, loved by him and having complete freedom to be themselves in his house. Worship with these children has to be simple; but they possess the great advantage of unselfconscious spontaneity; they are easily involved in a song or chorus familiar to them, the saying of rhythmical prayers, procession, lighting and carrying candles. These and other devices can make them at ease, occupied and content and convey to them and to their parents their acceptability and their ability to worship adequately if allowed to do so in their own way. The local acceptance of a severely subnormal child to baptism, confirmation, and communion can enhance this, and build upon a foundation laid in the more general context of the annual service.

Considerable progress has been made in recent years in the establishment of play groups for severely subnormal children. These present some difficulties, but are really no more complicated than for normal children, and the same regulations governing them apply. Some of the reasons for establishing them are different, but the needs of the children are the same as for any children. At present responsibility for SSN children still rests with the health authority but in the very near future, as noted above, this will be transferred to the education authority. It will be several years before the real effects of this transfer will be felt in the training centres. Training of staff, salary scales, and conditions of employment will need much careful working out before there will be real parity between the staffs of training centres and staffs of schools. In the meantime the needs of the pre-school or pre-training centre SSN child still have to be met. For the children the needs are materials and apparatus, attention being given to limited mobility of some children and the fact that physically more mature, and therefore heavier and stronger, children may be included in the group from time to time; social contact is needed with both adults and their own age group, and verbal training through ordinary, oft repeated speech, song, and rhythmic speaking. A day spent at a nursery for SSN children will be the best way of estimating some of the practical problems that will have to be solved. Staffing may present problems, but experience suggests that young people respond with alacrity to this particular form of service and provide much of what the children need. The qualification of the supervisor should be as for normal children and the help of parents on the rota basis will provide the involvement that is required of them.

For the parents the reasons for setting up a play group may differ slightly from those which would prompt the mothers of normal children. A handicapped child at home imposes a heavy burden of physical care. Some children remain completely immobile for a long time; the children are much slower in managing their feeding and toilet than their normal brothers and sisters. One of the characteristic effects of subnormality on some parents is an attitude of excessive concentration and over protection of the child, which can be emotionally as well as physically exhausting. A period of rest and relaxing of tension, a time during which the child can be weaned a little from mother's attention, a time when mothers can talk together or go shopping without their children, can be of immense value to both parents and children.

At five the children are eligible for the training centre provided there is one near enough and if transport is available for those who live some distance away. Not all children are able to attend. Closely associated with the training centre will be the local parent group, which is usually,

though not always, associated with the National Society for
Mentally Handicapped Children. Conditions at the training centre will vary from superb purpose-built units to bare
and ancient church halls. The association of the local minister with the training centre to which children from his
parish go will be as with local schools, a matter of personal
and tactful relationships in which he puts himself at the
supervisor's disposal and offers his own and his parish resources in any way that the centre can use them. The
training centre is the responsibility of the supervisor whose
name and address can be obtained from the local health
authority offices.

The parent societies vary from small groups meeting for
coffee and a chat to very active groups which raise money
for ambitious projects which meet the needs of the members and their children. Nursery schools, hostels, holidays,
and holiday homes are among the plans of most groups;
and the more active seek widely based sponsorship and support for their work. No community service undertaken on
behalf of the children and their parents should be planned
without the close consultation and cooperation of the
parent society.[1] It is through the parents that the most effective ministry to the SSN child can be achieved. If the pastor
can, by his preparedness to be involved in their situation,
and by his being seen to care through the parish's contribution to meeting their needs, then the relationship established with them will open the way for their response and
acceptance of his ministry.

THE EDUCATIONALLY SUBNORMAL CHILD

As we have said above educational subnormality is a technical term and should not, strictly, be applied unless there
has been a proper ascertainment of the child's abilities. But
it is also a generally used description of children whose

[1] For information about local groups contact the Mental Welfare
Officer or the Secretary, The National Society for Mentally Handicapped Children

backwardness is such that they need special attention at school and whose general educational attainment only reaches the level of children 20% younger than themselves. Such children vary from the very backward to those who are backward only in one particular subject and then often for some specific reason not directly associated with their general intelligence—such as maladjustment, which upsets their whole attitude to learning.

CHARACTERISTICS OF EDUCATIONALLY SUBNORMAL CHILDREN

Few handicapped children suffer from one handicap alone. Physical defects such as deafness, blindness, delicacy, epilepsy, and other physical handicaps, all affect learning. They affect the child's attitude to everything he does. ESN children are not unique in this respect and many suffer from another or several other sorts of handicap. Educationists recognize that the administrative arrangements for the children are very artificial and each child's difficulties are the result of a complex of deficiencies from which he suffers. An ESN child often suffers from additional defects of sight or hearing which are at first not recognizable if his chief defect is considered in isolation. His limited intellectual ability, as we can appreciate from what has been said about learning, makes it very difficult for him to handle any abstract ideas or language. Similarly simple instructions need to be given carefully so that the child can carry them out without too much effort or confusion; for example—not "John, will you please fetch the red book off my desk in my study" but—"John go to my study, look on the desk. You will find a red book there. Please pick it up and bring it to me." It takes a little longer, but the instructions are given in the order in which they are to be carried out. This is a great help. Backwardness in reading is common in ESN children and is often the result of lack of stimulation at home and the sense of failure—"I shan't be able to do it, so why bother to try?" There is similarly a difficulty in verbal self-expression and in understanding the spoken word; this results sometimes in seeking socially unacceptable methods of self-expression. Lack of self-control which accompanies emotional immaturity can make social relations difficult. This, combined with his slowness in grasping how to play a game or, once in it, being able to concentrate for only short periods, makes him unacceptable to other children, which increases his isolation and his will to strike back. Alternatively he may be frightened and withdrawn and incapable of doing anything for fear of doing it wrong or being rebuffed. ESN children tend to be very easily led; emotional immaturity combined with a sense of isolation and insecurity make them very responsive to attention. On the positive side this makes them very open to sympathy, understanding, and approval; they "blossom beyond belief in a sunny atmosphere".[1] On the negative side it lays them open to exploitation of all sorts by older and more mature children.

It is not necessary to spell out in any detail the pastoral implications of all this. These children need, above all, adult affection and approval, and acceptance by their peers. While the first should be taken for granted the second is rather more difficult to ensure. There has been much debate about the integration of ESN children into clubs for normal children. An enquiry directed to head teachers of ESN schools resulted in an almost equal view of the pros and cons of this. While most agreed that it was a desirable end to work for, it was liable to involve many difficulties on the way. It would be unfair to limit the activities of ordinary children in their own club by encouraging too many ESN members. (This view might justifiably be questioned in a Christian community.) On the other hand ESN children alone are inclined to lack initiative and organizing ability. Special clubs for the ESN are probably the best solution, but need plentiful adult support and the presence of a few normal youngsters who are aware of the problems and happy to participate in their solution.

[1] *All Children are Special*, A. H. Denney. C.I.O. 1967 (p. 28).

The unsuitability for these children of much of what passes as Religious Education for normal children is obvious enough. They highlight for the pastor much of what these pages have been trying to say about the need of all children for the experience of attitudes which they can sense and appreciate as being "good", and as leading to fulfilment rather than frustration, to acceptance rather than isolation, as expressing empathy rather than rejection. In this context of relationship Christ may be named and talked about, the traditional stories told, acted out, and retold, simple worship devised and felt as conversation with a living God; but these things will only be effective when the pattern of relational experience has been established. Every pastor, every adult Christian, who engages in work with mentally handicapped children must continuously refer himself back to the roots of his own spirituality and see the Christ he knows in the eyes, ears, and minds of the children he serves.

THE VICTIMS OF ADULT FAILURE

We have mentioned above that mental handicap and maladjustment have many causes and frequently these are to be found in the home background of the child. Such children come from many different home situations:

> There is the child of the father who drinks to excess or is a bully or is in or out of gaol; there is the child of the mother who is neurotic or deranged or feckless to the point of neglect; the child of parents who never work or who quarrel or who seldom speak to each other; the child from the home given over to sexual malpractices; the child who has by law been given to the virtuous mother, though it is the reprehensible father whom she loves; the home with conflicting loyalties; the home where there is prolonged illness; and, perhaps worst of all, the home which offers the child neither love nor security.[1]

As we have already shown it is impossible to separate the ministry to the child from the ministry to the home. Care,

[1] *Children in Distress*, Alec Clegg and Barbara Gregson. Penguin Books 1969

in these and many similar situations, is clearly shown first through work with the parents. In spite of this it would be defeatist to suppose that nothing can be done for the child outside home. What are the common denominators in these instances of home failure? Two seem to stand out clearly— that consistency of care which carries with it the sense of home as a secure and emotionally comfortable place to be, and that intimate affection between parent and child which always has room for praise and encouragement plentifully interwoven into the ordinary "do's and don'ts" of family life. Without these qualities, whatever else may be lacking, a child will suffer the fears and isolation which ultimately find vent in antisocial behaviour, withdrawal, or maladjustment of many sorts. If these qualities are present, poverty, squalor, overcrowding, malnutrition, can wound the child's spirit but will never kill.

The pastoral work of the Church in any place recognizes at least the Fatherhood of God and the Communion of Saints. Within this framework the Christian community holds together the weak and strong, the sick and the healthy. Within it the weak child should be able to find the strength of the mothers and fathers who know what true care really is. This is not to suggest that the Christian community should try to offer substitute mothering. This in fact it cannot do. But it can provide an experience of care and affection which will at least mitigate the lack of these elsewhere. School provides, if the child is fortunate in his teachers, another experience of the same sort; not a substitute for something else, but a reality in its own right. In a school in which education is seen as aiding the whole of the child's development, emotional as well as academic, there will be room for the expression of affection, praise, and sensitive compassion. When any community, small or large, is able to reveal in itself the fruits of the spirit, those who are part of it inevitably share in the "grace and comfort" which is thereby mediated. Here there is no substitute activity but the living presence of Christ himself, disclosed in the acts and attitudes of those who are his body.

CHILDREN IN TROUBLE

At the present time the future of the care and judicial systems that between them determine what shall be done about young delinquent children is under discussion. Any outline of these systems therefore may very quickly be out of date. Whatever is done in the future however, the financial implications of change are bound to make it slow in coming and it is therefore worth outlining the present situation. (See Appendix 2.)

THE JUVENILE COURT

Whatever changes are effected in the future, the juvenile court will be certain to remain part of the system of dealing with delinquency, though its terms of reference may change. At present it is concerned with children up to the age of seventeen. Its jurisdiction is divided into two age groups. Non-criminal proceedings can be applied for the whole age range up to seventeen, but for the age range ten to seventeen criminal proceedings may be taken. Whatever the nature of the proceedings, the juvenile court is a court of law and its conduct must conform to certain rules laid down by the Home Secretary. A degree of informality is however possible. The reason for which a child has been brought into court must be explained to him in such a way that he understands why he is there. Up to fourteen years of age, there is no right of trial by jury, but children between fourteen and seventeen may choose to be tried in a higher court if charged with an indictable offence. Proceedings are not open to the public and only those immediately concerned with the case are admitted. Names or other means of identifying a juvenile appearing in court may not be given in the press; the child's parents must attend the court and, if reluctant, can be compelled to do so.

In the course of the proceedings enquiries will be made about the child's background. These enquiries will relate to his home, his school, and his medical history. The local authority is responsible for supplying this information and does so through its various agencies concerned with children. The probation or child care service, or in some cases the child guidance service, will supply information about his home; the headmaster will be responsible for his school history; medical and/or psychiatric reports will be added if necessary. The purpose of all this is to be sure that the court posssesses the best possible foundation for exercising its responsibility for the welfare of the child. It is in this connection that the court is faced with a dilemma about its true function. The magistrates must, in every case, make a decision which maintains a balance between the demands of justice, the protection of society, and the best course for the child's future welfare, in terms of training, treatment, or rehabilitation. It is the attempt to meet this very real problem that has produced much of the argument about the changes that may be made in the future. The problem is by no means simple and, for the theologian and pastor, one that impinges upon a very wide range of his own particular and professional concerns. The interrelationship of sin, guilt, pardon, and renewal of life in forgiveness is something which will have occupied the parish priest in his own life and his theological studies. The interpretation of his thoughts about these things, to the distressed parents of a child to be brought before the courts, is not something that can be left to the spur of the moment. Parents are rightly concerned and often deeply disturbed about the social behaviour of their children. This concern is a point of contact with the Church's equal concern for the nature of man and the meaning of forgiveness as Christ taught it. The pastor needs to employ every possible way of extending parental understanding of their children's development and needs. Much could be said of the extent to which children reflect the shortcomings of their parents, their schoolteachers, and their pastors. The close investigation of the background of almost any child who comes before the juvenile court will throw into confusion every preconceived theory of guilt, blameworthiness, and punishment that we may have held, and compel us to question anew the practical implications of the Christian doctrine of *agape*.

PRESENT PROVISION FOR THE CHILD IN TROUBLE

Assuming a child has been brought before the court and the circumstances are clearly before the magistrates, what courses of action are open to them? As with adult offenders there may be *discharge*, absolute or conditional, *binding over* (which for children generally means that the parents will be liable for the payment of a determined sum of money if the child commits another offence within a specified period), *payment of fines*, or *damages*. Although these judgments may act as checks or deterrents they do not effect very much in the way of treatment or rehabilitation. Probation however does attempt both these.

PROBATION

A child may be placed on probation for up to three years. During this time, while still at home and so in his own environment, he will have frequent contact with his probation officer. The success of such a period of probation depends upon the sort of relationship that can be built up between the adult and the child. Much naturally depends upon the child's cooperation, but much more upon the expertise of the adult who understands not only the child's immediate needs but also the deficiencies of the home and surroundings from which he comes.

CARE OF A FIT PERSON

A fit-person order commits a child to the care of a fit person; most often this is the local authority. The child may be placed according to the facilities which the authority has to offer. He will of course be removed from his home and his home surroundings. A fit-person order therefore implies that the court feels these, or one of them, to be a threat to the child's wellbeing. The local authority will decide what may best be done for the child's welfare according to the available facilities; these will include the possi-

bility of foster care, admittance to a children's home, or
(through the local education authority) admittance to a
residential special school.

Not all children who are cared for by the local authority
child care services come to them through the courts; re-
ferrals may be made by schools, medical officers, police,
N.S.P.C.C., or even neighbours. The Children's Act of 1963
directed the child care service to act as a preventive as well
as a rescue service. But in spite of everything that a social
agency can do, ultimate responsibility rests upon the community to see to it that the many forms of breakdown
which bring a young person to court or to the children's
department are prevented from ever happening. Loneliness, isolation, ignorance, personal inadequacy, bad housing (or none), unemployment, poverty, and many other
causes produce the cynicism, despair, and desperation that
lead to family breakdown, cruelty, and neglect. Every community is a potential source of therapy for its members,
but this can only be made real by the sensitive participation of members in a policy of "good neighbours".

Removal to a children's home or to foster care places the
child in a new situation with new adults who are responsible for him. As soon as he is removed from home a new
set of problems face him with which he must deal as best he
can with the slender resources available to him. Deprivation
of one sort or another has almost certainly preceded his
arrival at his new home. He may have been the victim of
cruelty, desertion, neglect, or other forms of parental mis-
handling. He will not be easy to manage and whatever the
condition of home may have been he will resent being
moved from it. House parents and foster parents face a
hard and unremitting task in their exercise of care and
responsibility for deprived children. The children are not
a race apart, they are not "someone else's children"; they
are ours, they belong to the community which for many
different reasons has failed them. Their parents are someone's parishioners, their friends and school mates are in
someone's Sunday school, Youth Club, or house group.

Certainly the children come from outside the parish in which the home is situated, but the tracing of families, the follow-up of children, the regular visit to the home, an invitation to children and staff to come to parochial occasions, the encouragement of fostering, the maintenance of a constant flow of information and interest are the least that can be done locally.

It is, however, in the field of preventive work that the ordinary people can be of most help if they are conscious of other people's needs. Generally officials are not consulted until a family reaches crisis point: the child care officer will be asked to call when a mother is going to hospital: or she or the N.S.P.C.C. Inspector will be called in if a child is obviously being ill-treated or neglected; or the police will be called in when an offence has been committed. The best preventive work is done by ordinary good neighbours, who by their friendship and help can prevent these crises from ever arising, so that officials do not need to be involved.[1]

APPROVED SCHOOL

Children beween ten and seventeen may be sent to approved schools. The schools, "approved" by the home office, are not an altogether homogeneous group; some are run by the local authority, others are the product of philanthropic work of individuals or organizations, some have a religious origin. Each is responsible to a board of governors or managers who are concerned with staffing. In 1967, out of 121 establishments, 91 were under the management of voluntary societies or committees. In each school the headmaster sets the tone and very much controls the "policy" of the school; some schools have a full-time, some a part-time, chaplain. In the latter case this may be the local incumbent who may or may not be interested in the work of the school, or be fit or able to be involved in it. The children sent to approved schools are not all delinquent; some may be deprived children in need of care and protection. The choice of the school will depend upon places available.

The pastoral possibilities for those sincerely interested in

[1] *Children at Risk*, C.I.O. 1968 (p. 42).

working with approved school children and staff are immense. But it is probable that in many schools it will be quite as much with staff as with children that the pastor will be concerned. However, with these children as with any children, the problems of community acceptance will loom large in any plans that are made. Most children in approved schools have suffered more or less severe rejection at home and/or in the community from which they have come. To them and to their parents they have been "put away". Much of the schools' work will be an effort to restore both their self-respect and their sense of responsibility to society. This sounds a pompous phrase, but since the child is in a school it is *his* responsibility as a citizen which he is being taught, either formally or more adventurously, according to the nature of the school. The role of the pastor is here again that of a member of a community which has the duty of acceptance laid upon by its Christian vocation. The interpretation of the child to the community and the practical demonstration of his acceptance must be the background of parochial policy. No community that calls itself Christian can dare to add to the experience of rejection the child has already suffered. Staff and children alike will need to be made aware that this acceptance by the local community is a reality and must be given the opportunity of experiencing it.

In addition to these three possibilities before the magistrate, each of which has a curative purpose as well as a disciplinary one, mention should be made of the Attendance Centre to which children over ten may be sent. They are usually required to attend for periods of one or two hours during their spare time, for up to a total of 24 hours. Centres are usually run by the police and run on lines of good discipline and useful instruction. Detention Centres are only available for children over fourteen. Sentence is normally up to three months and consists of a sharp reminder to the offender of the error of his ways. Borstals are not immediately available to the juvenile court and committal must be by a higher court. They are only available to children of fifteen or over. Remand homes are now generally used as places of temporary stay pending reports or observations required by the magistrates.

THE FUTURE

Future policy for children in trouble will undoubtedly reflect much of the thought and research which has accumulated over the last decade. What form legislation will take is not yet clear, nor is it clear, even when the legislation exists, just how it is going to be implemented. Staff and finance dictate any policy, however good it may be in theory, and recruitment to the social services concerned with children should be taken just as seriously, by those who have the opportunity, as recruitment to the teaching profession or to the ministry. Even when staffs are adequate the work of social agencies is largely and inevitably taken up with "ambulance" work, and prevention is bound to take second place. This is where the pastoral role of the Church really comes in. The Church in any place, that is the Christian body of all denominations, must be sensitive to the needs of the community of which it is a part, albeit a small one. Its greatest asset, after the possession of the faith itself, is perhaps its ability to be articulate and active, to be a "go" Church as well as a "come" one, to be a listening Church as well as a speaking one, to seek as well as hoping to be sought. By being this sort of body it may exercise a "compassionate awareness" of society which will enable therapy to be exercised without too much self-conscious effort.

A very experienced child care officer (speaking of the welfare office envisaged in the Seebohm Report, para. 590) writes:

> Children in trouble cannot be isolated from other children or other social problems. They are not an island unto themselves. Therefore, eventually we must aim at turning our welfare state into a welfare caring community.[1]

[1] J. W. Freeman in *Children in Trouble*, Conference Report. University of Leeds Institute of Education 1968

7

Partners in Ministry

Throughout this book the word "pastor" has been used to indicate the minister of the parish or a member of his staff. It would, however, be absurd to suppose that the pastoral ministry is the exclusive preserve of the ordained staff of the parish or of its paid lay servants or voluntary officers. The pastoral ministry is the responsibility and function of every Christian regardless of his or her other day-to-day occupations. Ministry in this context is a term that includes the service given by every Christian in the name of Christ. No parish priest can exercise a parochial ministry alone. Fortunately he does not have to. He has at hand the lay members of the community who are concerned with the many aspects of its life. It will, however, often fall to the professional clergyman, as it frequently does to the social worker, to be the initiator of a pastoral programme or policy within a parish.

We drew attention in the last chapter to what is there called "a therapeutic community". This must not be understood in too technical a sense; the word "therapeutic" here does not mean any more, though indeed not less, than the evangelical precept to bear one anothers' burdens. This is put well in a paper by Muriel Smith of the London Council for Social Service:

> Today technological change is always bringing new social problems, but with greatly improved social conditions the emphasis is not so much on the needs of deprived districts and the problems of social breakdown, however serious, as on the creation of a social environment which gives support to those in difficulty and prevents such problems from arising.[1]

[1] *The Social Workers*, B.B.C. 1965.

This suggests perhaps that in a community which contains a small proportion of persons with clearly defined needs the therapy is a one way affair in which the needy are constantly at the receiving end. This is too limited a view of community for a Christian to accept, and certainly not one which will help to clarify the laity's role in the pastoral care of children. Children are not by any means the constant receivers and it is important that they should not be so regarded. Just as any process of small group therapy is a matter of interchange between group members, so the therapeutic nature of a Christian community is a constant giving and receiving by all members.

The place of children within the community is determined very much by the fact of their being children. They are dependent and cannot escape their dependency, but this does not mean that this fact must always dominate their relationships with adults. Children must be recognized by the Christian community as being an essential element in it, the absence of which would impoverish the community. It is frequently the care and consideration for the young, with the restraints and disciplines that it imposes, that enriches the nature of a community as it does of a family, by the love, unselfishness, and self-discipline that it engenders. It is for this reason that much good will ensue from the close involvement of adults with the children's work of the parish and the equally close integration of children and young people into the activities of the adults. The capacity of children to serve, to work hard for something they see to be valuable, to be loyal and courageous in the face of criticism and difficulty, is often severely underrated by adults to their considerable loss as well as that of the children.

Similarly underrated is the sensitivity of many adults to the needs and natural inclinations of children. This is frequently so when the ministry to the children is seen in the limited context of Sunday School teaching or junior club. Important as both these parts of children's work may be, they are only a part and those who teach in the Sunday School or help at the club are usually people with certain well-defined abilities, or they should be. There are many lay people, in women's organizations, men's societies and clubs. on the P.C.C., or just members of the church and no more, who would be thoroughly intimidated by being asked to help in either the Sunday School or the club, but who would find no difficulty and much pleasure in the presence of three or four children in their house or garden, toolshed or workshop, for an hour or two one day a week; who would enjoy explaining how to strip and repair a three-speed gear on a bicycle or cut a plank of wood straight with a saw, make sweets or cut out a dress pattern. Sitting around the television and watching some special programme and chatting about it afterwards does not need the sort of expertise usually associated with teaching or organizing a club evening, but it can often achieve quite as much or even more in the process of making a reality out of the term "a Christian Community".

Parochial church councils which are reluctant to spend money upon children's work, or which seldom give more than a perfunctory few minutes to the discussion of parochial policy for the children, adopt this sort of attitude because they are totally disengaged from the younger members of the parish, have no direct contact with them, and feel no responsibility for them. Such attitudes are a denial of the unity of Christ's body and the relatedness of the members of the Christian family. For more than a century now western society has been encouraged to take too introverted a view of the natural family and has seemed to forget that this was not the view of the Gospels. It has been found in voluntary work concerned with children that the most effective contribution, the greatest initiative, lies with those who are involved in the situation, who face the very problem that the work sets out to tackle. The many parent-centred societies that have grown up in recent years to meet the needs of handicapped children, to improve educational conditions, to get a fair deal for children and parents from the hospital services, have all been the result of immediate adult involvement with the particular problem. This same principle governs the ministry to children in any parish. It is essential that parents of a wide age-range of children in the parish should be strongly represented at the policy-making level. Without them discussion will be theoretical and lack adequate knowledge of needs to be met and appropriate ways of meeting them.

In a west country parish with a sizeable new estate a group of parents constitutes the children's committee of the parochial church council. This committee is responsible for the organization and financial administration of two play groups. It employs and pays a part-time qualified infant teacher (married with young children). It co-opts to its membership representatives of two parent organizations (N.S.M.H.C. and the Muscular Dystrophy Society). It hopes soon to see parent organizations of this sort joining together in order to gain more members for interchange of know-ledge and experience. The committee has regular personal contact with the local social workers and there are always members available to visit the children's ward of the local hospital, which is some miles away from the parish. The committee, meeting monthly, has several other matters on its Agenda including the finances of the Sunday School, for which it is responsible to the P.C.C. and to whom it reports current needs and special expenses.

It is difficult to see how any P.C.C. can hope to deal adequately with children's work without this sort of delega-tion. Another parish, much larger and near London, has a full time children's officer responsible to a very competent committee and undertaking the training of Sunday School teachers, helping the team of clergy with their work with children and acting as a play group supervisor three morn-ings a week. She is a professionally trained teacher.

Whatever pattern of administration is decided upon or whatever financial arrangements are possible or impossible, the pastoral care of the children must include the parents and must be seen as a joint operation of the whole body ministering to the needs of its members.

THE STATUTORY SERVICES

This is no place for a discussion of the relationship between
the clergy and the social workers. This has been done elsewhere and reference should be made to these sources.
(*Crucible*, March 1968. *The Church and the Social Services.*
C.I.O. 1969.) There are, however, certain points coming
from the discussion which seem to need stress. First, as we
have mentioned elsewhere, the pastor comes to his people as
a man of God and a man from God. He does not represent a
social work agency, to reflect some present social policy or
(except very occasionally) to disburse financial relief. His
attitude to people relates to an eternal not a temporal situation. He comes to bring the love of God and the sympathy of
the priesthood (Hebrews 4. 15) to those who call on him
rightly expecting it, or to those he calls upon because he
thinks they need it. He may or may not possess the skills of
a professional counsellor, but he should possess all the knowledge of the human personality that his learning and experience can provide, because he is dealing with human persons
for God. This lays a responsibility upon him which he cannot avoid. To know "what is in man" is as fundamental a
part of the pastor's training as knowing what is in the doc-
trines of the faith. Theology and life are complementary
and one without the other is barren. (It will frequently be
the case that the need of people is recognized as being
beyond what the pastor himself can offer and he will then
call in the help of the professional case worker.)

The second point is well summarized in *The Church and
the Social Services* (para. 19):

> While Christians in the social services may be convinced that
> their activities are as much part of the life of the Church as its
> organized worship and witness, it can be discourteous if they
> refer to this belief in situations where it may be interpreted as
> a claim that all good works in our modern, pluralistic, secular
> society are dependent upon the fact that, whether it is recog-
> nized or not, people are still living on "Christian capital".[1]

[1] Op. cit., para. 19.

One regrets this attitude of "Christian capital" since presumably the Christian, using the analogy, would prefer to regard the Holy Spirit's work as a current account rather than a capital deposit. The fact remains however that an attempt which seems like a take-over bid by Christians for all that is "good" is not acceptable to people who conscientiously reject this source for their actions. Tact and readiness to accept others' viewpoints must govern relationships with social workers if these are to be fruitful. Our constant thankfulness to God for all his goodness at every eucharist we celebrate should not make us unable to accept convictions other than our own.

The third point is made by David Wainwright at the end of a discussion of interprofessional roles (*Crucible*, March 1969):

> ... A good exercise is a short conference where equal groups of clergy and social workers meet, define their roles, and then examine these definitions critically in the context of a case study. Encounters of this sort can feed back into the church a new appraisal of the role of the clergy *vis-à-vis* other professional colleagues.

The pastor concerned with children's work will find immense value in such occasions for interprofessional discussions, and not only, of course, for his work with children. Not every Children's Department is prepared to see the pastor's role as complementary to its own, and such meetings can prepare the way and help to confine territories to areas of common concern and cooperation. An example dependent upon such relationships occurred in the case of Margaret, the sixteen-year-old member of a family closely associated with the church. There were two children of the mother's first marriage, of whom Margaret was one, and one from the father's first marriage, and one of the present union. Margaret, an intelligent and likeable girl, became very independent after her elder brother left home to take up a job a considerable distance away. In a fairly short time she became a considerable anxiety to her mother on account of the relationships she was forming, and it was difficult to persuade her father to accept responsibility for her and take seriously the possible consequences. He regarded such suggestions either as exaggerated or matters which did not really demand his attention. There was, as may be imagined, a very complicated pattern of family relationships. Although nothing had so far happened that demanded a call upon social service, the family clearly needed outside help. Pastoral care was always present in the situation, but it was help from beyond the locality which was really needed. A discussion of the case with the probation officer resulted in a call from a very experienced member of his staff who was able to strengthen the family ties and help them through some difficulties that lay ahead.

Another occasion illustrating help operating the other way was Olive's family. Though she was quite well known to the local parish priest, there was not such a close relationship as is indicated in Margaret's case; the family were not church members or in any church group. A call made by a member of the probation office staff however led to a visit to the family who freely discussed their troubles. Olive had been involved in what amounted to little more than adolescent pranks, but the young people (aged all under fifteen) had been reported by some over-solicitous citizen for indecent behaviour. They were eventually placed on probation and little damage was done. Olive's sister (aged twelve) was however deeply affected, having the feeling that the family was in terrible disgrace. She refused to go to school and would not go about the village without her mother or father. It took some three months for her to recover herself completely, but this would not have been achieved without the cooperation, quite unconscious, of children associated with church groups. The climax came with an entirely uninhibited discussion of the original incident in which Olive was involved ending in it being a "good laugh". So far as the children were concerned the "over-solicitous citizen" was the one who was henceforth "in disgrace", suggesting that sometimes the judgment of children is more just in its appraisal of society than that of the processes of law.

VOLUNTARY SOCIETIES

Every pastor will be aware of the existence of voluntary societies working within his cure. Each will have a different purpose and will be trying to channel the voluntary work and the money of the community towards the realization of their particular goal. For this practical reason alone there is bound to be an element of competition not only for money but also for the limited time that people can give outside their working day. There are a large number of voluntary societies working for children—so many, in fact, that a separate directory of them has been found necessary. Clearly cooperation with such societies is far better than competition and coordination is desirable wherever it can be brought about.

A group of organizations likely to be of value to pastoral work is that of parent-centred societies which attempt to meet the needs of children through their families. Local branches of the N.S.M.H.C., the Spastics Society, societies for the deaf, blind, muscular dystrophy, rubella, and other severe childhood handicaps, all aim at informing, helping, and strengthening the parents to cope with the handicap of their child. It will be an elementary part of pastoral care to have a list of all local personnel involved in the work of these societies and a list of H.Q. addresses which will supply local sources of information is given in the Notes on Chapter 6 (pp. 113–14). Through personal acquaintance with regional and district officers of the major societies the way will be opened for local contact with both parents and children. The annual meetings of societies are open events and opportunities of meeting the persons most involved locally; very often monthly meetings are also open and clergy are welcomed. There are many questions that parents ask, but baptism and admission to communion of children who present physical difficulties may be tackled as problems for which real and immediate solutions can be found. Discussion and instruction on these topics can lead to fruitful discussion over a much wider front.

It is always worth bearing in mind that one important aspect of voluntary work is its relationship to the community as a whole. It is easily assumed by many people, including good Christians, that the caring community is essentially the professional social workers who are paid by the community to do this job on its behalf. While there is, of course, some truth in this, it is not enough for the Christian who recognizes that the work of caring is as important as the care itself. A community satisfied with this interpretation is a community which has bought itself out of Christian living and may be compared with a person who is prepared to send a substantial freewill offering to the treasurer of the P.C.C. but never joins the "body" at worship or at work. It is the Christian recognition of "good neighbourliness" that has produced the good-neighbour schemes which are a feature of parish life in many places today.

CHILDREN AND COMMUNITY SERVICE

In recent years there has grown up an awareness that children and young people are very capable of involvement in community service. Schemes effecting this have spread downwards from the V.S.O. schemes for young people which operate in one form or another in many countries, to groups of children in secondary schools actively meeting local needs according to their abilities and interests. Fortunately the skill and experience of people engaged in this work are coming to light in published form and we have no excuse for not being aware of what there is to do and how it can be done. Not only is the work beneficial to those for whom it is done, but it is also of great educational and moral value to the children involved. To enable children to see need and be moved to make some attempt to meet it is a better lesson in Christian responsibility than any number of good lessons or projects which can only touch the issues at second-hand.

CARING THROUGH WORSHIP

A child care officer once remarked to me that while she realized that a sense of isolation was a necessary part of her professional position in the community (the only C.C. officer in a large rural area) and must be lived with, she also felt as a Christian a sense of isolation which was not really necessary. At the celebration of the eucharist that she regularly attended the cases much on her mind were always a large part of her "intention" and she wished they could be shared sometimes with the rest of the congregation. This was a clear indictment of the irrelevance of much that is offered in far too general terms for congregational participation (a situation which is much improved by the flexibility of Series II). But it would represent a substantial advance in every parish if one celebration a week were devoted to the needs of local children and names were submitted to the parish priest each week for special inclusion. Every professional and voluntary worker, every distressed parent, indeed the children themselves, could be assured that at one special time their needs, concerns, and difficulties were being placed before God in their local church.

8

Children in Hospital

The visiting of children during even a brief stay in hospital is an important part of pastoral work. This may probably be taken for granted, but what is often given less attention is the preparation of children for hospital and the helping of parents to handle the period of separation and the period immediately following return home, in a way that meets the children's needs. The following remarks by a senior consultant in child psychiatry will illustrate this. He is speaking of research carried out in America and goes on to illustrate a similar situation in England:

> As with the children, so with their parents; in this series of 100 cases, 47 of the mothers were found to be quite hazy about the nature of their child's illness. They claimed that no adequate explanation had been given them by their own doctors. A much larger number (76) claimed that nobody had bothered to explain to them, in terms they could understand, why their child required to be in hospital at all. Not surprisingly, therefore, all the parents were anxious to some degree, 57 exhibited pathological anxiety about the implications of hospitalization for their child, and this anxiety was reflected in the patient's unsettled and insecure state.

The writer continues to cite examples of children's anxieties which result from lack of factual information and proper preparation:

> One nine-year-old boy told Dr Vaughan that he was trying very hard to keep awake all night, because his mother had told him the operation would be done while he was asleep.

> An eight-year-old boy was moved from the main ward into a cubicle because he had suffered from post-operative vomiting. No explanation had been given to him for this change and

Dr Vaughan found him intensely miserable. He explained he thought this was a punishment for having been a coward before his operation because he cried a little.[1]

It is clear that the parents and the child must, in this as in so much of the ministry to children, be considered together. The routine visiting of the children's ward must be combined with attention to the work with families back at home; the facilitating role of the minister is again important and the many sources of help among those professionally concerned must be tapped. But before suggesting the sort of programme for parish groups that this implies something must be said about the children who go to hospital.

SEPARATION AND ANXIETY

We have already pointed out the dangers that separation from home brings with it. These are specially evident with very young children. Some years ago James Robertson made a detailed study of two-year-old children in hospital for comparatively brief periods. From his researches it became very clear that such children suffered much more emotional stress than had been supposed. He showed that what normally passed as a "settling down" period was in fact a time of strong resentment at separation from mother and passed into behaviour which indicated, not a "settled" child, but a child with all the symptoms associated with the sort of "withdrawal" that accompanies deprivation.

Added to the evidence of Robertson's research (which has gone on to include the effects of fostering and of residential nursery care) was that of the 1959 Report of the Platt Committee on the Welfare of Children in Hospital, which strongly recommended unrestricted visiting and the provision for mothers to accompany their very young children to hospital. Although by no means fully implemented these two documents have brought about a very substantial change in the last decade.

[1] *Children in Hospital: their Education and Welfare.* Papers given at a conference at the University of Liverpool. 1965.

The most vulnerable age is between one and two and the effects of hospital stay after returning home reduces with age. Of course this reduction of after-effects is the natural result of development and the possibility of providing proper explanations of what is being done. It should not, however, lead us to suppose that all is well simply because the child is older and able to understand what he is told. Even if separation is accepted and he knows that he will soon be home, a child still worries about himself, about what is going to happen to him, and about what is happening to the other children in the ward. The greatest remedy for worry is activity.

Play in hospital is receiving increased attention, and the functions it can perform are many. Not only will carefully organized play activities keep the child's mind off brooding anxiety, but freedom in play will provide opportunity for the self-expression which helps to neutralize or "play out" anxieties. With older children a play-leader, without any strictly "hospital" role, will be recognized and treated as someone close to home and ordinary life and so a suitable confidant with whom to "talk out" the things that are worrying and mysterious. Play-leaders and teachers between them are able to be not only friends in need who understand and sympathize but also conveyers of accurate factual information which allays much of the anxiety that comes from ignorance or misleading hints of what happens in hospital. Though strictly outsiders they are nevertheless inside and so can be relied upon to be "in the know".

At the time that the Platt Report was receiving official attention a group of mothers in London was setting about the formation of a parents' society to bring pressure to bear upon hospital authorities to extend their visiting facilities. At first this group took the name of "Mother Care for Children in Hospital". Their activities included the encouragement of hospital play groups as well as agitating in many ways for unrestricted visiting for parents. Later the name was changed to the National Association for the Welfare of Children in Hospital and their membership was extended to persons professionally concerned with sick children. They now have many groups scattered over the country and give much help and advice on many matters connected with sick children. The information and financial support of play leaders in hospitals is a matter for local action; advice can be obtained on how to set about forming play groups. Help is also given to parents in preparing their children for hospital. The local Association can be a valuable link between the pastor and the parents of sick children. If a local branch does not exist the formation of one by an interested and able lay member of the local Christian community will be a valuable adjunct to ministry.

VISITING CHILDREN IN HOSPITAL

The above remarks will be some guide to the approach that the pastor will make to the sick child. He will be aware of the strains the child is undergoing, the anxieties about what is going to happen to him. He will recognize the need to reassure the child about himself, his home, and the care and competence of the nurses and doctors whom he sees around him.

Visiting children who are unknown to the pastor may be valuable if an open and reassuring attitude is taken. He will come from outside, will have no anxieties associated with him and be a welcome break in what can be a damaging boredom. But visits should always be prepared in advance whenever possible. The parents of the child should be visited well in advance and seen, if possible, together. Their anxieties may be discussed and understood so that fears about himself that the child may have gleaned from them may be understood and clarified. The home, the child's room if he has one of his own, his toys, should be known well enough to be subjects of conversation. If it is possible to take some small thing from home, to borrow a familiar game to play, to take a familiar book to read, or the latest copy of a favourite comic, it will all help to break through barriers and enable the child to express himself freely. Messages from friends, news of their doings, what is going on at school, a note or message from his class or class teacher will help to make him aware that he is remembered, wanted back, and eagerly waited for in the normal world he may feel has deserted him.

Before talking to the child himself a short chat with the sister will provide some idea of the child's immediate condition and determine roughly how long the visit should be, whether there is time for a story or a game, how able he is to sit up, to handle toys, pencils, plasticine, and so on. Very young children need often the assurance of a hug or kiss which will convey more than words; often they are quite inarticulate when faced with even the most familiar adult other than their parents.

Children will often like to, indeed may for the first time really want to, say their prayers. Children known to a visiting parish priest may be asked if they are doing this, and the way in which they are doing it may be discussed. Thinking about friends and home in relation to the loving care of God can be strengthening. Cards with written prayers are available from several sources and often used as "something to take him". But they can be restricting in their objectivity. Some card or picture to look at as he thinks about those for whom he is praying may be more useful. It is also most valuable for a child to be asked to pray for another child who is sick, particularly if he is in the same hospital or ward.

Finally it is well to remember that most hospitals have a whole or part time chaplain who knows the staff and will be ready to discuss the needs of individual patients with their parish priest and will include children in his rounds in either visiting or administering the sacraments. Clearly every pastor will need to make the acquaintance of the chaplain of his local hospital and will consult with him regularly concerning both child and adult patients.

CHILDREN AND DEATH

It may happen, though fortunately today very rarely, that a pastor will need to minister to a child who knows that he is

dying. Only the personal sensitivity of the priest and his
intimate knowledge of the child will enable him to do this
adequately. Even without this knowledge there are things
that a skilled pastor will be able to do and say to convey an
understanding of the eternal love of Christ for us and our
need to trust in him.

In 1967 the late Simon Yudkin, a well known consultant
paediatrician, wrote in the *Lancet*:

> It would be wrong, I am sure, to assume that every ill child is
> frightened of dying and discuss the issue with all of them, but
> the truth is that we are often unaware that a child is frightened
> of dying, either because it seems inconceivable, or because we
> will not allow ourselves to think about it. The answer surely
> lies, in part, in being more aware of the possibility that a child
> might be afraid of dying. But we must also try to recognize
> symptoms which may indicate a child's deep anxiety about the
> possibility of death. Depression and a lack of interest in
> ordinary daily activities, out of keeping with the effects of the
> illness itself; unprovoked anger and resentment towards his
> doctors; resentment towards his parents of a child old enough
> not to be affected by the mere separation in hospital—these all
> suggest anxiety about death. We should also be suspicious
> when a child tries to deny symptoms which are clearly present
> —a method of defence against anxiety about death which
> adults also use. Some children who are not very ill may appear
> not to be satisfied with a relatively simple explanation or re-
> assurance, or they may look at the doctor quizzically whilst the
> explanation is going on, as if daring the doctor to tell them
> the worst.
> If we become sensitive to these signs, we may be able to help
> a child voice his fears and we may even, with some experience,
> voice them for him.[1]

The recognition of the symptoms of anxiety may, alas,
come too late for anything sufficiently effective to be done.
But the fact that the anxiety exists is something that may be
foreseen in the whole process of pastoral work with children.
It is easy for us to lose sight of death in our work with the
young, simply because, in our western and relatively secure

---

[1] *Lancet*, 7 January 1967. "Children and Death" (republished in
Man's Concern with Death, ed. Arnold Toynbee, Hodder and
Stoughton, 1968) should be carefully studied by every minister.

world, it is remote. But this is no reason for its avoidance. Children should be encouraged to discuss its implications for Christians while they are in good health, so that, for facing this anxiety as for other problems of living, they have a base from which to set out.

SUGGESTIONS FOR PAROCHIAL ACTION

In the parish itself the best work can be done with parent groups. Membership by a group leader of the National Association for the Welfare of Children in Hospital will ensure that members are kept up to date with the ways of preparing their children and themselves for hospital. They will also have a ready source of help and advice on any matters relating to the care of their children when in hospital. Parochial support for a hospital play group or, as already suggested, the initiation of such a group, can also be guided by advice from the Association. The cooperation of the consultant paediatrician and the hospital matron are essential to any work in connection with the hospital. In one parish in which the parent group invited the matron to come and talk to them about the hospital the young children were invited back to the hospital, shown the children's ward, and met members of staff. If any had subsequently been admitted it would have been to a place already familiar and to the care of people who were not complete strangers. Invitations to hospital staff should ask that they come in uniform; it is often the uniform which children in hospital find frightening.

Visits to the parish, both to parents and children, by members of hospital staff can be arranged through the matron and is obviously a valuable way of breaking the ice, but a visit to the hospital itself is even more valuable.

The organization of a regular visiting panel to ensure that every child is visited during visiting periods may seem impractical in a large parish, but should at least be the aim. If the hospital is some distance from the parish transport will be a constant problem; therefore a small team of car owners to cover this, as well as other occasions of need, is a constant parochial asset; but petrol must be paid for and this should be understood in all arrangements made. It is often a wise thing, if use of this service is frequent, for journeys to be recorded and settlement to be made through the treasurer of the P.C.C. or other appointed person.

The help of the hospital chaplain and/or the medical social worker will enable the parish priest to check entries from his parish and these, if not visited, should at least receive a card (these are available from church bookshops) and, if they are in for more than a week, a personal letter from the parish assuring them that they will be remembered at the appropriate service on the following Sunday. If such letters are printed they should at least be personally signed by the parish priest.

Going to hospital may well be the most traumatic experience in a young child's life; every effort should be made to give support to both him and his parents.

9

Immigrant Children

Experience of a specialist ministry to immigrant children is necessarily limited to areas of immigrant settlement and to the comparatively short time that such distinct minority groups have become a feature of modern British society.

There are, however, certain aspects of work in areas of immigrant residence that emerge as guide-lines for the future. It is probable that for some time to come churches will find themselves increasingly concerned with two particular ages—the pre-school children and the school leavers. For our purposes it is the first of these that need consideration. Clearly the principles of pastoral care for these children will be the same as for any children. But, because of certain social factors and attitudes, emphasis may have to be laid on particular parts of normal care. For example, a much higher proportion of West Indian mothers work than their native British counterparts, though the gap narrows year by year. Further, because of the housing problem in areas of immigrant concentration, the number of pre-school children needing play facilities tends to be higher for each area than for a proportional area of native housing. There are other factors which likewise demand different emphasis—language, social customs, religious customs.

Families or individuals who have come to Britain from overseas of their own free will have generally done so to find work and a higher standard of living. Many of those who have come from Asia hope eventually to return when they have made enough money for them to set up business or practise a profession in their native country. Those who have come from the West Indies have come to stay and to make their home in what is to them the "homeland". To secure a job and a place to live is for them good fortune; it is something they could not do at home. For many the worst of British conditions is better than the shanty towns of home. They often feel homesick, especially for the climate and the close-linked social life of home, but they also, particularly the men, see themselves as "lucky". For the children however it is not a home that welcomes them. The British way of life is for them inhibited, complex, and introverted—the noisy party, the birthday celebrations, the street dances are all frowned upon by their white neighbours. The "good luck" of their parents is "bad luck" for children who scarcely remember "home" except as infants or who, born in this country, hear of it only from the conversation of parents, who are liable to speak of it at times of homesickness or frustration as a place to be looked at through rose-coloured spectacles. The children are soon made conscious of the problems of their parents and the attitudes of white neighbours, and are at the receiving end of the worst of both.

The two cultures of the immigrant from overseas and his British neighbour will always present difficulties, whether the immigrant comes from Ireland, Cyprus, West Indies, or Pakistan. There are religious differences, different attitudes to marriage, different eating habits, different clothing, different sorts of social grouping with their attendant patterns of behaviour. Cultural differences cannot and should not be minimized or glossed over. They must be recognized and understood. The immigrant child will frequently want to reduce to an absolute minimum the differences between himself and his British counterpart. He will often tend towards being assimilated rather than integrated. It is important that he should have the option in this matter and that neither one nor the other should be forced upon him. Whatever his choice, or his compromise, it must be assisted and supported. The conflict that he experiences within himself is the reflection of the conflicting attitudes of the adults around him and his own self-abnegation is born from the hostilities with which society surrounds him. This is not the place to discuss these matters, as they extend far beyond the pastoral care of the children. Their solution can only be found in Christian values as they apply to persons and a real effort to disseminate knowledge of one another that will at least aid the process of mutual understanding. The following notes do no more than highlight some significant points of difference or possible friction. Further information will be found in the reading list for the chapter.

THE WEST INDIAN

Two features of West Indian life need emphasizing, because failure to recognize them has led to much misunderstanding: first the West Indian family, and secondly the related matter—the attitude to marriage. British society, in common with western society generally, thinks of the family in biological terms, that is, those related by blood and, most particularly, those of first and second degree of relationship. The British family is mother, father, and children, with the inclusion, according to circumstance, of grandparents. The following description of the West Indian family illustrates a quite different idea, which the writer describes as the functioning family:

> A typical group (household) could consist of a grandmother, her grown-up son and daughter, her daughter's illegitimate child, and a niece she had brought up since her sister's death. The family income is derived from the son's earnings outside the home, the woman's cultivation of a plot of land, and spasmodic maintenance payments for the child, from his father, who is now married and living somewhere else.[1]

When West Indians emigrate they naturally tend to reproduce in the host country the patterns of social life at home. The extended family is the source of social life and enjoyment, the means of ensuring security, the nursery of the young members. Without it those brought up in the West Indies feel isolated and vulnerable. The re-creation of it in

[1] *New Backgrounds*, ed. R. Oakley. OUP

Britain results in what are sometimes called ghettoes and indeed may sometimes earn the name from circumstances of housing availability beyond the immigrants' control. But an understanding of the strength drawn from the extended family and its inner life may help the neighbours of such groups to bear with the difficulties it can create in the very different society of the host country. Integration will often have to be the task of second and third generations rather than those who have known an upbringing rooted in the social patterns of "home".

The attitude towards child rearing is largely the result of the sort of grouping described above. Responsibility for children depends upon many different things and not just upon the fact of fatherhood. A child in West Indian society is seldom brought up in the home of both parents. But this is not so disastrous as it might be for a British child, since a wide range of relatives will be available among whom he will be able to find adequate parent substitutes. Within a single community the adult population as a whole feels responsible for the community's children. This means that, though a child may often find his immediate home disturbed, he will almost certainly be able to find another that will care for him within the community. Changes in the home result often from the indeterminate attitude to marriage. Marriage is expensive and concubinage cheaper and easier and more free from specific obligations. Whoever may be the woman with whom a man lives, he assumes responsibility for her children whether by him or another man, but may treat very loosely his responsibilities for children by a previous union.

All these facets of family life are liable to undergo radical change and stress in the new immigrant situation in Britain. While the West Indian will try to reproduce home patterns when he first settles, obviously it is impractical for the whole group to migrate together and the norms of western society will pressure him towards early marriage and assimilation to a way of life which will confer social status on the immigrant.

The success of integration is largely dependent upon the host society tolerating what appears deviant until second and third generation children have overcome the stresses which a two-culture system forces upon them.

The West Indian's religion is Christian, with a fair proportion of Anglicans from those dioceses in which the work of Anglican missionary societies has been strong. Most immigrants are "protestant". But their Protestantism is more of the sort associated with pentecostal groups in this country than with the well known free church groups. Worship is far less formal and liturgical than forms familiar to British churches; it is warm, enthusiastic, conversional, and encourages congregational response and participation.

The West Indian child is accustomed to a fairly rigid though often inconsistent discipline. Parental expectations of educational performance often exceed the abilities of the child, and progressive methods at school are seen as "soft". There is little understanding of educational method and hence there tends to be a gap between parent and teacher which is hard to bridge. Self-discipline is rated highly and what would be regarded as normal play or untidiness in an English child might easily meet with severe reprimand or punishment in a West Indian home.

In spite of all these and many other cultural and social differences the children of West Indian parents are moving fast towards integration since only thereby lies independence, progress, and happiness for the immigrant. But the process contains strains and tensions which it must be the responsibility of the host societies to ameliorate as far as possible.

INDIAN AND SIKH IMMIGRANTS

After the partition of India into Muslim Pakistan and India, the areas adjoining East and West Pakistan, namely, the Punjab and Gujarat, were severely unsettled by a flood of refugees. It is principally from these regions that Indian immigrants come. The motive, as with the West Indians, is mainly economic. The Sikhs are affected by the steady break-up of large land holdings, which leaves sons of large families without an economically workable inheritance. Indian families from East Africa, however, come for political rather than economic motives, being ousted by the policy of Africanization from the areas in which they live.

The most important factor in Indian settlement in Britain is the kinship group. The Indian comes to a family already established, who will house him and find him accommodation; he leaves behind a family to which he is still very closely tied and which may well have contributed substantially to the cost of his travel from India to Europe. Family, in this context, extends through several grades of blood-relationship to the village kinship relations. Settlement in England places considerable strain upon the complicated kinship groupings and relationships, but the home pattern is duplicated, as far as possible, when members settle in Britain.

Sikhs do not have the same close affiliations of kinship, but are bound together by a deep attachment to a common faith and the use of a common language. In recent years their faith has, through the teachings of the ten *Gurus*, and particularly by the work of the last—Gobind Singh—formed them into a very real brotherhood which is strongly resistant to outside pressures. Their temples (*gurudwaras*), several of which have sprung up in England, are both places for the study of their faith and community centres.

The Indian family has several very important differences from the nuclear family to which we are accustomed in the West. Within the family itself the closest relationships are between mother and son and between brother and sister. These are reflected in the responsibility felt for the care of the aged members of the family. This is imbedded in the kinship network, beginning with the sons and daughters and extending to the limits of relationship.

Marriage, in spite of Indian government legislation, is most often still a matter of family arrangement, marriage even being possible between a man in Britain and a girl still in India. Religion and place of origin are the most important considerations, a wife being chosen usually from the village of her husband or from one geographically and socially associated with it. The girls are carefully vetted to make sure that they will fit into the life of the family.

Although Indian women do not traditionally work outside the home, this is something which is changing not only among immigrant women in Britain but also in the towns of India. From about five or six years old boys and girls tend to be segregated to assume their sex roles. The girls are trained in household duties while the boys learn the ways of the outside world. Firm discipline is maintained by the parents and the role of each member of the family is clearly understood.

Education can produce tensions in the immigrant family. School in Britain is, against Indian standards, excessively permissive and undisciplined. Indian children expect to learn by rote and to be passive receptors of the teacher's instruction. They are not expected to "find out for themselves"; more progressive methods are not understood by the parents. School may well be seen as a threat to traditional ways of life and behaviour. In spite of this, Indians place a very high value upon education, particularly for boys, and will make considerable sacrifices to ensure that it is successful.

Sikh and Indian (Hindu) children adopt comparatively easily to their new surroundings. The Sikhs do not eat beef and, especially in the first years after arrival, may insist on retaining their turban and long hair. The Indians often, though not always, retain native clothing, but are less insistent on this matter than their Pakistani Muslim comrades. Hindu festivals are colourful and interesting and their description and meaning are useful ways into mutual understanding.

In general both Sikh and Indian desire a high degree of integration but also want to retain their own culture and not have it swamped by westernization. The situation they seek is similar to that of the Jew, who is scarcely distinguishable from his native neighbour yet retains his social and religious culture without allowing it to become a matter of conflict.

PAKISTANI IMMIGRANTS

The majority of Pakistani immigrants come from rural areas, but the time is coming when most entrants to schools will have been born in this country and an urban environment will be natural to them. In the first instance it was the men and boys who emigrated and settled in all-male communities. The women were sent for as jobs and a more settled way of life made it possible. Their arrival accentuated the native way of life in this country and aided the creation of distinct Muslim communities. Many characteristics of Pakistani groups are similar to those of Indians. The kinship grouping is based upon strong family and village relationships, reinforced by religious sanctions. In spite of some degree of modernization the Muslim women are still tied to the house and seldom play any active community role. The practice of purdah which includes total veiling is undergoing considerable modification, but clothing is still regulated by the principle of showing no more of the body than face and hands.

It is the men who establish the family's contacts outside home, including the school. Boys identify with this role from an early age. Conditions among immigrant families in Britain often make it difficult to re-create the home family network and this can result in the isolation of women. Girls are carefully protected, so far as this is possible, from outside influences. This produces considerable strain within families and can make adjustment very difficult for the girls who see, at school, the very much greater freedom of their British friends.

The Muslim faith is much more demanding in terms of social conduct than either the Hindu or the Sikh and the provision of religious instruction is an important means of combating the influence of western culture particularly upon the girls. Education is highly valued, but is seen as challenging tradition. Regulations about clothing cause difficulties over PE and swimming at school—difficulties that not every school is prepared to meet with the sympathy and understanding shown by Spring Grove, Huddersfield.[1] As with other immigrant groups, the permissive element in English education is not understood and discipline is regarded as slack even when at its best. The Muslim home is very clear about the roles of each member; parents expect obedience and respect, which they feel are being undermined by the attitude of teachers and English friends.

The family, religious feasts, the wearing of traditional clothing, the tunic (*kemise*) and trousers (*shalwar*), the observance of food regulations (fasting and not eating pork), are all factors making for stability and security in the difficult task of adjustment to life in Britain. To deny the Muslim child the right and the opportunity to adhere to them is to cut him adrift from his own culture and his surest social support. The result of such an attitude could be disastrous to an already complex enough task.

Enough has been said to make it clear than any approach to pastoral work in immigrant communities needs both tact and understanding. There is frequent reference to the "problems" of the immigrant and much effort is made to solve these supposed "problems". We have mentioned elsewhere the need for community education in understanding children and their needs. Frequently the "problem" lies in those who need to understand quite as much as in those who need to be understood. The Christian should be the first to recognize that most problems of relationships in human societies require self-questioning by both sides. The pastor will recognize the need for constant "educating" of himself and his people of whatever colour, race, or religious persuasion in those things that lie behind all human relationships and go much deeper than the present "problems" of either group.

[1] *Spring Grove—the Education of Immigrant Children*, Trevor Burgin and Patricia Edson. OUP

ORGANIZATIONS THAT HELP

There are several organizations in existence which concern themselves with various aspects of race relations, but three will be found to represent official action, however, inadequate, to promote policies which reduce tension and aid understanding.

The Race Relations Board. This has been set up to deal with the legal problems arising from the Race Relations Acts. Its powers are limited and it depends very much upon public support for its proper operation. Breaches of the law which forbids racial discrimination can be reported to it and most are dealt with through conciliation councils at local level which have to examine the pros and cons of each case brought before them. The functions of both Board and Councils are clearly defined and they cannot step outside the legal remit given them.

The Community Relations Commission and local Community Relations workers. The Commission and its officers have the hardest task of all as they represent the only official organization aimed at solving the very many problems that arise at local level and at the same time being intimately involved in the larger issues at national level. As yet there is not specific training or terms of reference for a C.R. officer. He may be white or coloured, his area may be any size and contain anything from one to thirty thousand immigrants. He will have to rely mainly on the central organization for expertise and support, and both central and local financial aid is minimal. The Commission is supported by the Home Office but is not a government department and must justify itself if it is to continue to exist. However the local worker, who is appointed and paid by the Commission, has a local council to support him, but this support is not always wholehearted or necessarily informed. But the officer will be the best local source of help and information. He will have much expert knowledge of the

local situation and have given much thought to the race
relations issue. He will be in touch with other groups among
both natives and immigrants and have considerable personal
experience to aid his judgment. In return he needs help.
This should be both moral and, when necessary, outspoken,
especially on issues to which a specifically Christian attitude
may be expected.

The Institute of Race Relations. This is essentially a research organization concerned with all aspects of race at
home and abroad. But it has naturally concerned itself very
much with the home situation and the need for accurate
documented research in a rapidly changing situation. In
1969 the small *News Letter* which had been issued monthly
by the Institute for some years past was replaced by *Race
Today*, a monthly publication which should be read by all
those whose pastorate includes racial minorities.

10

The Child and Worship

WORSHIP AND EDUCATION

The education of children whether at school, at home, at Sunday School, or in clubs or groups has a forward look somewhere within it. Schools not only hope to develop the child's personality and inform his mind according to his age and ability, but must also attempt to equip him for adult society and, possibly in his last years at school, for some specific form of employment. Young people are given insight into future problems of home and community life, of adult relationships, of managing their personal affairs. The school curriculum maker keeps one eye upon the developmental needs of the children and the other upon the expectation of the adult society of which they eventually become members. Home is less concerned with the future until school leaving is in sight, but none the less the social norms to which the child is made to conform are those of the adult society with which his parents identify themselves. Some parents have a tendency to keep children back from too early excursions into maturity; they feel that childhood is all too short and should not be bitten into by the demands of the future; others prefer their children to be dependent, and feel at a loss when faced with vigorous and self-assertive independence.

Sunday school has a dual function so far as education is concerned. Its terms of reference are necessarily limited; it is designed and is expected to teach religious knowledge. This can be interpreted as referring to Biblical and theological facts or to the way in which people communicate with God through prayer and worship. In these respects it coincides with the function of the RE lesson in school. In addition the Church is expected to inculcate attitudes and beliefs and train the child in worship. It is also expected to provide the sort of situations in which children may practice worship as well as learn about it. Some of these functions are attempted also in school, particularly in the voluntary schools. But generally the educational purpose of the classroom takes precedence over what is justifiably regarded as the function of the local Christian community.

Clubs, holiday courses, day conference, house groups, and other forms of the educational ministry to children out of school have the same sort of roles as the Sunday schools for which they are often preferred alternatives. There is often time set aside for worship, as well as instruction or discussion about it.

In all these situations education and worship are closely linked. There are however dangers in this association of functions which are not always recognized. A glance at the many forms of worship provided in appropriate books for school, club, evening meetings of one sort or another, or even for Sunday school show clearly some of these dangers. Most of these fall into a common pattern. There is a reading of scripture or other writing (poetry or prose) which opens a theme. This is followed by prayer in which petition and thanksgiving are included and there are usually one or two selected hymns. Prayer is sometimes meditative, sometimes formal; there may be recorded music. Such patterns as this,[1] of which there are many variations, have ample justification in their liturgical origins and, at certain levels of religious development, may fit admirably the needs of the children with whom they are used. They also have the advantage of being available in their completed form for the leader to read or direct without overmuch prior preparation. Their repetition makes them familiar to the children, who soon learn to know what to expect and

[1] A list of books suitable for use with children is given in the Book List on p. 115.

appreciate the element of familiarity. What then are the disadvantages of these forms?

First the fact of prior composition, very prior if they are in printed forms, militates against relevance. They cannot be immediate in their theme, nor can they relate to the widely differing capacities and developmental stages of the children. Even at their very best, with proper attention to language and originality and interest of source, they are imposed forms which assume just as rigid a pattern as any adult liturgical service. They are, in fact, adult in conception. This is not to say that they are invalid for the children or unacceptable. But it is well to recognize that they are often more effective, as "educational" rather than "worshipful" exercises.

Some forms of this sort have other dangers within their content which must be looked for carefully. Prayers are frequently composed which suggest things of adult choice which the children are required to pray for or for which they are to be thankful. This may be perfectly in order; on the other hand it may easily become a way of stimulating the child's conscience or "getting at him" under the guise of prayer. When a child is really thankful for a happy evening with a pal or just the television and the chance to buy an ice cream or chips on the way home from school, he is often faced at morning assembly or at the children's service in church with thankfulness for the goodness of his parents and the wisdom of his teachers. That it is the last two factors which have, in various ways, made the other things possible is a step in adult conceptualizing which the young child cannot, and should not, be expected to make. Similarly petition for certain virtues, which the child may see as what "sir" or parents really want, can with some imagination be rendered in a concrete manner which is more relevant to the thoughts and feelings of those on whose behalf the prayer is said. Recently published collections of prayers and readings for various occasions recognize these facts and a more imaginative approach to worship seems to be on the way. A recently produced collection of worship/lessons[1] has shown how, at sixth-form level, education and worship can be combined so as to make an effective contribution to both. The combination is deliberate and overt and far preferable to the ambiguity of some earlier forms. It is to be hoped that others will apply this principle lower down the age range.

EXPERIENCE AND WORSHIP

What has so far been said of formal patterns of worship which are prepared or selected in advance is not intended to preclude their use. In situations such as school assemblies (about which something has already been said) or children's services they are the only means of corporate worship which can try to cover the needs and ways of expression of widely separated age groups. The difficulties they present can be reduced to reasonable proportions, and intelligent adaptation can often help to overcome their seeming irrelevance and tendency to impose on the children themes or attitudes that are foreign to them. There are however other ways of remaining within a traditional framework but yet preserving a spontaneity not possible with forms taken from manuals.

What we have learned of children's ways of thinking at different stages of development suggests strongly that worship will have most chance of succeeding when the group is developmentally homogeneous. This may, under some circumstances, be difficult to arrange, but it is a good reason for replacing school assemblies by worship in classes on some days each week. In Sunday school, worship in departments also eases the problem; final prayers and blessing can still be corporate, but be kept very brief.

A second important necessity of worship, if it is to arise from the children themselves, is the relationship between the children and the group leader. This must be free and informal if there is to be real communication, and in this

[1] *Education through worship*, A. R. Bielby. S.C.M. Press 1969

operation real communication is essential. Further, the group must not be too large; twenty is a practical maximum. If it is larger than this it is best to break it into small groups of two or three, each group taking the part that one child would take in a smaller group. If preparation is going to be adequate major acts of worship should not be too frequent, perhaps once a week at school, twice a month in Sunday school. On intervening days or Sundays prayers may be brief and formal and make a link between children's and adult worship. Such suggestions as these may be felt to be so far removed from the demands of the Education Act of 1944 that they are not practicable in school. However several schools are encouraging experiment on a once a week basis, other days conforming with the usual pattern of assembly. Sunday school and similar voluntary church groups are of course quite free to experiment.

The first stage in linking worship with the experience of the children is to discover what their experiences are. There will be common experiences such as those dependant upon the seasons, local events or the local housing, work or leisure patterns which govern community life. But there will also be a wide range of personal experiences which will need careful discovery and sifting; the success of this will depend upon the relationship the group leader has established with the children. Two or three periods of informal discussion will probably be necessary before the children have decided upon those personal items which they are prepared to release for group use. Sensitivity by the listening group leader will elicit significant experience which should be selected for direct inclusion in worship and the unexpressed feelings which should receive attention without being made overt. For example John may have recently moved into the neighbourhood and begun at school only a few weeks ago. This is open information for inclusion by John; the leader will be aware of the unexpressed sorrows of leaving old friends behind and the fear and anxieties about holding his own in a new school and making new friends.

After the opening up of the experiential matter to be used the leader will need to provide a framework into which the act of worship can be fitted. This will probably include the traditional elements of thanksgiving, reading, hymn-singing prayer, and praise. Only the framework should be offered; the content of each part and the order of presentation may be left to the children to devise. The leader may help with the discussion, particularly the categories into which the children's different sorts of material will fit; he may also help the less articulate to express themselves. He will use his knowledge of the children and his own expertise in encouraging appropriate children to select music or take part in dance, mime or drama which may form part of the worship. He should at the time make quite clear that, although there is a final "performance" being planned, the whole process of preparation is itself an act of worship, a struggle with themselves and with God, to establish communication which is true to themselves and worthy of God.

The following paragraphs express very well the value of non-verbal communication which is perhaps the most spontaneous and expressive of all ways children have of saying something. Such forms can really come into their own when the whole action is a Godward movement of the children without the interposition of any other agency.

> Movement is a language which the ordinary person may use more easily than any other to express those feelings, ideas, and experiences which transcend words. Some of the mysteries which surround and pervade human life, some of the spiritual realities which we said at the beginning are the essence of religion—the feeling of awe and wonder, a sense of the miraculous and the supernatural, a sense of God—may be both glimpsed and manifested in expressive dance. . . .
>
> All creative arts have within them something of the divine, and dance more than any has the power of immediate communication. It is an art which the most awkward and clumsy, the least gifted and the most graceless, can take up and make their own. Some brightening of beauty and of grace is bound to come, and within it will be at least a little of the spiritual.[1]

[1] *Lord of the Dance*, V. R. Bruce and J. D. Tooke. Pergamon Press 1966

WORSHIP AND MYSTERY

The appropriate aims and intention of religious education in state schools might be summarized in words attributed to F. W. Sanderson, who was headmaster of Oundle School from 1872 to 1922: "We must march boys up to the frontiers of the unknown." "The frontiers of the unknown" are the growing point of human knowledge, the limits of human achievement. It is at the frontiers of the unknown that we touch mystery, that man meets "God".[1]

Our deepest battle, whether in the sophisticated west or the bewildered "older" cultures, is not to scout superstition—which science well enough can do—but rather to build sanctity, and to do so without withdrawal from the world and without exemption from man.[2]

These two quotations would be good ones upon which to end this short account of pastoral ministry as between them they sum up what the purpose of our work with children really is. A sense of mystery in the world of material things is the beginning of religious thinking and spiritual growth. It is the refusal to stop short at the objectively knowable and to reach out towards the unknown on both this side and the other side of death. As Smith goes on to say, the Christian faith is in a life lived and a death died, and in a new life beyond death which is the measure of the worth of the life lived. We have a natural tendency to avoid the discussion of death with children, to see life as positive and death as negative; yet such an attitude is scarcely proportionate to the treatment both are given in the New Testament. It is an emasculated version of our faith which insists upon treating the resurrection and the whole Easter feast solely in terms of the present, the "new life", in which we hope to participate more fully when we know "even as we are known". Here is the greatest mystery before which, in spite of its familiarity, we all personally tremble. In the twentieth century, which has seen death on a vaster scale

[1] *Religious education in the Secular Setting.* J. W. D. Smith, SCM Press 1969
[2] *The Privilege of Man*, Kenneth Cragg. ULP 1968

than ever before, it is a forbidden subject. Yet to avoid it entirely in our work with children is to shy away from the mystery which is at the centre of the Christian faith.

Kenneth Cragg asks for sanctity. He asks that we may be humble and holy but not withdrawn, not a new sort of respectable "drop outs". Sanctity springs from humility and humility from a recognition of the transcendence of God and the vastness of the trust he has committed to us.

Mystery and sanctity are both hard to express adequately in words; they are the stuff of art and poetry, of personalities, attitudes and "being" which defy description. Children have the right and the need to live with the best of human culture, both in the things they see and hear and feel and the people with whom they work and live and enjoy themselves. All this is the stuff of worship, the approach to the unknown, the participation in the holy; it is the real goal of the pastoral ministry to children.

Books for Further Reading

The following list of books, which is arranged under the chapters to which they relate, is a short guide to further reading. Many of the books included in the list have their own bibliographies which can carry the study of the subject a stage further. In selecting these books, price and availability have been kept in mind, and all the books mentioned are written for the general reader rather than the expert. In many instances further information is obtainable from the organizations whose addresses are added to the chapter lists.

CHAPTER 1

COX, E., *Changing Aims in Religious Education*. S.C.M. 1966
GOLDMAN, RONALD, *Religious Thinking from Childhood to Adolescence*. R.E.P. 1964
HYDE, K.E., *Religious Concepts and Religious Attitudes*. Educational Review Vol. 15
LOUKES, R., *Teenage Religion*. New Ground in Christian Education. S.C.M. 1965
MADGE, V., *Children in Search of Meaning*. S.C.M.

CHAPTER 2

BOWLBY, J., *Child Care and the Growth of Love*. Penguin Books
ERIKSON, E.H., *Childhood and Society*. Penguin Books 1965
FLETCHER, R., *The Family and Marriage in Britain*. Penguin Books
LEE, R.S., *Your Growing Child and Religion*. Penguin Books 1965
NEWSON, J. & E., *Infant Care in an Urban Community*. Penguin Books
— *Four Years Old in an Urban Community*. Allen & Unwin 1968
WINNICOTT, D.W., *The Child, the Family and the Outside World*. Penguin Books 1964
YOUNGHUSBAND, E. (ed) *Social Work with Families*. Allen & Unwin 1965

CHAPTER 3

EYKEN, VAN DER W., *The Pre-School Years*. Penguin Books 1967
HARTLEY, R.E., FRANK, L.K. and GOLDENSON, R.M., *Understanding Children's Play*. Columbia University Press 1952
HOSTLER, P., *The Child's World*. Penguin Books
MATTERSON, E.M., *Play with a Purpose for the Under Sevens*. Penguin Books 1965
MILLAR, S., *The Psychology of Play*. Penguin Books 1968
MOLONY, E., *How to Form a Playgroup*. B.B.C. 1968
TRASLER, G. and others. *The Formative Years*. B.B.C. 1968
YUDKIN, S., *0–5: A report on the care of pre-school children*. National Society of Children's Nurseries.

ADDRESSES

The National Association of Pre-School Play Groups
87a Borough High Street, London, S.E.1

Nursery Schools Association
89 Stamford Street, London, S.E.1

CHAPTER 4

BEARD, R.M., *An Outline of Piaget's Developmental Psychology*. R.K.P. 1969
BORGER, R. and SEABORN, A.E.M., *The Psychology of Learning*. Penguin Books 1969
BREARLY, M. and HITCHFIELD, E., *A Teachers Guide to Reading Piaget*. R.K.P. 1966
PIAGET, J., *The Language and Thought of the Child*. R.K.P. 1962
SANDSTROM, C.I., *The Psychology of Childhood and Adolescence*. Penguin Books 1968
THOMPSON, R., *The Psychology of Thinking*. Penguin Books 1959

CHAPTER 5

(See list under Chapter 1)

CRAFT, M., RAYNOR, J., COHEN, L. (eds.) *Linking Home and School*. Longman 1967
GREEN, L., *Parents and Teachers*. Allen & Unwin 1968
HILLIARD, F.H., LEE, D., RUPP, G., NIBLETT, W.R., *Christianity in Education*. Hibbert Lectures 1965, Allen & Unwin 1965
SMITH, J.W.D., *Religious Education in a Secular Setting*. S.C.M. 1969

YOUNG, M. and MCGEENEY, P., *Learning Begins at Home*. R.K.P. 1968

The Fourth R: The Durham Report on Religious Education. S.P.C.K. 1970

Religious Education—A Bibliography for the Use of Teachers. C.E.M. 1966

Parent–Teacher Relations in Primary Schools. Education Survey 5 H.M.S.O. 1968

ADDRESSES

The Secretary, Confederation for the Advancement of State Education
9 Addison Road, Gt. Ayton, Middlesbrough, Teeside

The Hon. Secretary
The National Federation of Parent-Teacher Associations, Garnham House
189 Stoke Newington High Street, London N.16

The Director and Field Officer, Home and School Council
Derwent College, University of York, Heslington, York, YO1 5DD

The Church of England Board of Education
Church House, Dean's Yard, Westminster, London S.W.1

The National Society
69 Great Peter Street, Westminster, London S.W.1

CHAPTER 6

CAVENAGH, W.E., *Juvenile Courts the Child and the Law*. Penguin Books 1967

CLEGG, A. and MEGSON, B., *Children in Distress*. Penguin Books 1969

DENNEY, A.H., *Children In Need*. S.C.M. 1965

— (ed) *Children at Risk*. C.I.O. 1968

— *All Children are Special*. C.I.O. 1967

FURNEAUX, B., *The Special Child*. Penguin Books 1969

JACKSON, S., *Special Education in England and Wales*. O.U.P. 1966

KELLMER-PRINGLE, M.L., *Caring for Children*. Longman 1969

MAYS, J.B., *Education and the Urban Child*. Liverpool University Press, 1962

SEGAL, S.S., *No Child is Ineducable*. Pergamon 1967

ADDRESSES

National Bureau for Co-operation in Child Care
Adam House, 1 Fitzroy Sq. London W.1

National Council of Social Service
26 Bedford Square, London W.C.1

Church of England Board of Social Responsibility
Church House, Dean's Yard, Westminister, London, S.W.1

The Guild of Teachers of Backward Children
7 Albemarle Street, Piccadilly, London, W.1

The Elfrida Rathbone Association, Toynbee Hall
28 Commercial Street, London, E.1

National Society for Mentally Handicapped Children
86 Newman Street, London, W.1

The Association for Special Education
19 Hamilton Road, Wallasey, Cheshire

Invalid Children's Aid Association
4 Palace Gate, London, W.8

The National Association for Mental Health
39 Queen Anne Street, London, W.1

CHAPTER 7

DICKSON, A. & M., *Count Us In*. Dennis Dobson 1967
RUSSELL, K. and TOOKE, J., *Learning to Give*. Pergamon 1967
KELLMER PRINGLE, M.L. (ed) *Directory of Voluntary Organizations concerned with Children*. Longman 1969
YOUNGHUSBAND, E., *Social Work and Social Change*. Allen & Unwin 1964
The Social Workers, B.B.C. 1965
The Caring Community. National Council of Social Service
The Church and the Social Services. C.I.O. 1969
A Guide to Voluntary Service. H.M.S.O. 1969

See addresses for Chapter 6.

CHAPTER 8

AUTTON, N., *Pastoral Care in Hospitals*. S.P.C.K. 1968
NOBLE, E., *Play and the Sick Child*. Faber 1967
ROBERTSON, J., *Young Children in Hospital*. Tavistock Publications 1958

ADDRESSES

Church of England Hospital Chaplaincies Council
Church House, Dean's Yard, Westminster, London, S.W.1

Save the Children Fund
29 Queen Anne's Gate, London, S.W.1

CHAPTER 9

BANTON, M., *Race Relations.* Tavistock Publications 1967
BURGIN, T. and EDSON, P., *Spring Grove; the education of immigrant children.* O.U.P. 1967
BUTTERWORTH, E., *A Muslim Community in Britain.* C.I.O. 1967
HASHMI, F., *The Psychology of Racial Prejudice.* Pamphlet published by C.R.C.
STAFFORD-CLARK, D., *Prejudice in the Community.* Pamphlet published by C.R.C.
HILL, C., *Immigration and Integration.* Pergamon 1970
HOOPER, R., *Colour in Britain.* B.B.C. 1965
MASON, P., *Common Sense about Race.* Gollancz 1961
OAKLEY, R., *New Backgrounds.* O.U.P. 1968
ROSE, E.J.B., *Colour and Citizenship.* O.U.P. 1969

ADDRESSES

Community Relations Commission,
Russell Square House, London, W.C.1

Institute of Race Relations,
36 Jermyn Street, London, S.W.1
MONTHLY PUBLICATION: *Race Today*

CHAPTER 10

BANYARD, E., *Word Alive.* Belton Press 1969
BIELBY, A.R., *Education Through Worship.* S.C.M. 1969
— *Sixth Form Worship.* S.C.M. 1968
BROTHER KENNETH, *Live and Pray.* C.I.O. 1970
BRUCE, V.R. and TOOKE, G.D., *Lord of the Dance.* Pergamon Press 1966
CAMPLING, C. and DAVIS, M., *Words for Worship.* Arnold 1969
HOBDEN, S.M. *Explorations in Worship.* Lutterworth 1970
JONES, C.M., *School Worship.* University of Leeds 1965
KITSON, M., *Infant Praise.* O.U.P.

PRESCOTT, D.M., *The Junior Teachers Assembly Book*. Blandford Press
— *The Senior Teachers Assembly Book*. Blandford Press
ROSE, M.E., *The Morning Cockerel Book of Readings*. Hart Davis 1967
QUOIST, M., *Prayers of Life*. Gill 1965

ADDRESSES
Bernard Brayley
The Lornehurst Service
191 Creighton Avenue, London, N.20

Appendix

RELIGIOUS EDUCATION IN SCHOOLS

The following notes are a very brief guide to the legal relation-ship between the clergyman and the church school.

AIDED SCHOOL

The Church of England aided primary school will have six managers, four of whom are churchmen. The parish priest is usually the chairman of the managers. A Church aided secondary school will have two-thirds of its governing body appointed by the Church. The incumbent or a suitable person appointed by the managers can teach regularly in the school; the teaching may be denominational and the children may, on special occasions and in accordance with local regulations, worship in church. All the teachers are appointed by the managers and governors. (For full information on all matters connected with Aided Schools see *The Aided Schools Handbook*. Canon L. B. Tirrell. National Society and S.P.C.K. 1969.)

CONTROLLED SCHOOLS

The Church of England controlled school will have two managers or one-third governors, appointed by the Church. One will usually be the incumbent and the other(s) will be appointed by the Diocesan Education Committee on the recommendation of the P.C.C. These are called Foundation Managers. Denomina-tional teaching may be given for only two periods a week and then only to children whose parents have asked for it. The in-cumbent may give this teaching himself. If there are three or more teachers on the staff the Local Education Authority must ensure that one is appointed, approved by the Foundation Managers, to give this teaching. He will be called a "reserved teacher". Opening worship must be in accordance with the Trust Deed of the school, and this will almost certainly be Church of England. Provided the managers agree the parish clergy may conduct the worship. The children may not be taken to church for normal worship, though special services, preferably out of school hours, are often taken in church. All appointments of teachers are the responsibility of the L.E.A., but the managers are consulted. No questions may be put about religious allegiance of teachers. Finance is entirely the responsibility of the L.E.A.

COUNTY SCHOOLS

Children who are members of the Church of England may be given instruction in a withdrawal class if the parents request it and if the church and the school can arrive at suitable arrangements to make it possible. It must be regular and should complement the agreed syllabus being used in the school. Before making themselves responsible for a withdrawal class the parish clergy must be sure of their ability to carry it out efficiently.

CHILDREN WITH SPECIAL NEEDS
NEW REGULATIONS

Since this chapter was written new legislation has appeared which makes changes in the legal and care procedure for dealing with children who come before the juvenile courts or who need care, protection, or control. Details of these changes which will begin to be implemented in 1971 can be found in the White Paper *Children in Trouble* (Cmnd. 3601. H.M.S.O. 1968) and the subsequent legislation, *The Children and Young Persons Act 1969*. (H.M.S.O.)

The main changes so far in operation are as follows:

1. There will be no prosecution of children under 12. Children between 10 and 12 can be taken before the courts as in need of care, protection, or control and may be placed under a care order. This will be executed by the local authority.

2. A care order may be extended, if thought fit, to children and young persons between 12 and 17.

3. Children under 12 can be supervised by the local authority; young persons between 12 and 17 by the local authority or a probation officer.

4. The approved school order will cease and the range of local authority provision will be comprised in Community Homes, statutory and voluntary, under Joint Planning Committees.

Index

BV
639
C536
D399   Denney
          Working with
     children

12001

BV
639
C536
D399

12001

    Denney
       Working with children

DEMCO